'I have been waiting for this boo
pastor and leadership team shor
remarkable man and here his gi
for every leader. I have known M
is the best communications dire
Jesus and the Church, and is pa

C000146904

This is not a book on church media; it is a manual for church mission.'
Simon Ponsonby, Pastor of Theology, St Aldate's Church, Oxford

'Mark Crosby is the real deal – a man with a passion for Jesus Christ and a gift for helping churches communicate it.'
Mark Elsdon-Dew, Director of Communications, Holy Trinity Brompton, London, and Alpha International

'This book is so helpful, practical and accessible from a master of the craft. It is for all those who would love tips on how we can communicate better to both the Church and the world around us. Over the years, I have watched Mark do this brilliantly with the minimum of fuss and the maximum of grace.'
Mike Pilavachi, co-founder and leader, Soul Survivor

'As the Communications Director for Vineyard Churches (UK & Ireland), Mark has been hugely effective in shaping communication both within and beyond our movement across multiple platforms. His passion for Jesus and the Church, his strategic mind, and his diligent study of current and emerging means of communication combine to make what he has to say well worth listening to. In this book Mark demonstrates his flair for making the complex simple, providing practical tips that have the potential to transform the Church's ability to connect with those within and far beyond it.'
John and Debby Wright, National Directors, Vineyard Churches UK & Ireland

'The work of community formation is progressed through reliable communication. My friend Mark Crosby excels in leading churches to communicate in healthy ways that help rewrite the story of their cities. *So Everyone Can Hear* will be an invaluable tool for all churches seeking to grow in strength as they gather and scatter for the sake of their communities.'
Alan Scott, Anaheim Vineyard, USA

'A clarion call for churches to use all the communication tools the twenty-first century has to offer in service of reaching the world with the gospel. Compellingly written, beautifully designed and grounded in Mark Crosby's extensive experience, *So Everyone Can Hear* is a gift to all Christian communicators.'
Jo Swinney, Director of Church Communications, Christian Publishing & Outreach

'Church communications is one of the vital ingredients that we need to learn how to master as church leaders. Mark is one of the leading thinkers and practitioners in this field; I have known him for a number of years and it's a delight to now have his experience neatly packaged in a book. *So Everyone Can Hear* is a vital addition to the toolkit of every church leader.'
Jay Pathak, Senior Pastor, Mile High Vineyard, USA

'Mark is one of those great disciples who quietly make things happen and don't mind who gets the credit. He has been such an encouragement in helping his church and many others communicate to students and young adults; he joins up conversations and people all the time. From my experience in working with churches looking to reach students, I know it is mission-critical to communicate clearly and relationally, and to follow up with consistency and kindness. Mark does this in his own life and so I pray this book helps many others do the same in the hidden and public spaces of following Jesus and being his Church.'
Miriam Swaffield, Fusion

Mark Crosby is the Director of Communications for Vineyard Churches UK & Ireland and serves at Vineyard Church, Cardiff. He also trains church members in Europe and the USA about how to communicate in healthy ways.

SO EVERYONE CAN HEAR

Communicating Church in a Digital Culture

MARK CROSBY

First published in Great Britain in 2019

Society for Promoting Christian Knowledge
36 Causton Street
London SW1P 4ST
www.spck.org.uk

British Library Cataloguing-in-Publication Data
A catalogue record for this book is available from the British Library

ISBN 978–0–281–08214–8
eBook ISBN 978–0–281–08215–5

1 3 5 7 9 10 8 6 4 2

Designed and typeset by Mark Crosby
Printed in Turkey by Mega Print

eBook by Fakenham Prepress Solutions, Fakenham, Norfolk NR21 8NN

Produced on paper from sustainable forests

CONTENTS

A NOTE OF APOLOGY

Over the past two decades, I have made copious notes on talks I've heard, books I've read, items on the radio, tweets, conversations, podcasts and films. The notes are rarely verbatim and have been reworked after personal reflection and refined for training notes; they've been rewritten again for this book and then edited in subsequent drafts. When I can remember specific people who have inspired me, I have credited them, and I believe I have done so in every instance. If I have failed to do so, I apologise; it was not my intention to miss anyone out. If we have ever sat together and talked, and you saw me scribbling notes, it is likely that you inspired me and that your words have percolated in me and been used to create something in this book. I'm grateful to everyone who has spoken truth over my life; it has helped to bring this book into being.

FOREWORD

If you were to ask us about 'church communications', we would quickly point you to Mark Crosby. Whether being trained on how to use social media, communicating digitally with a movement of church leaders, or (heaven forbid!) even updating a website, we have sometimes found ourselves out of our depth in the murky world of communications and have needed this very talented man to save us from ourselves!

What Mark so excellently demonstrates in *So Everyone Can Hear*, and what he has often demonstrated to us, is that all leaders have a role to play in communicating church within our current culture.

Mark shows how church communications help to lay the foundations for the health and growth of the local church, starting with vision, values and prayerful planning. Technology has provided opportunities to build on such communications, approaching them slowly and sustainably, not frantically in fits and starts.

Whether you are a church leader, a small-group leader or are launching a new ministry, this book is for you. It will guide you to a greater understanding of how you can make use of the myriads of tools available to you in order to reach not just your church but also your surrounding area. *So Everyone Can Hear* is a practical, inspiring and helpful guide for every leader in the Church, no matter his or her age, stage or experience.

We have always believed hugely in Mark and all that he does to serve and equip the local church. This book is an invaluable resource, which we are delighted to endorse; we are confident that it will be a great blessing to you.

At the end of the day, what is the Church – a community of Jesus lovers – without communication at its heart? And what is our mandate in the world? To share the gospel in such a way that everyone can hear.

John and Eleanor Mumford
Vineyard Churches Global Coordination

I dedicate this book to all the unseen heroes who faithfully serve behind the scenes.

THIS BOOK

How Churches Should Be Communicating in the 21st Century: if you've ever written a dissertation, you'll know just how many times you say your title over and over. This was mine. And now, more than 15 years since I finished my Marketing and Public Relations degree, it continues to be my passion. How can I help churches make the most of the tools at our disposal to reach our towns and cities with the love of Jesus?

These past years have seen a seismic shift from traditional media and printing presses to a digital culture in which information is instant and connection is a finger swipe away.

The Internet is a canvas on which we can paint a picture of God's love. It's a printing press to issue invitations. It's a library for us to tell better stories. It's a noticeboard to keep people updated. It's a gateway into our communities. It's a spoon to stir the pot, keeping everyone included.

Jesus will build his Church and he invites us to join him. As those he calls friends, we journey with Jesus, we cooperate with what the Father is already doing, and we walk in step with the Spirit.

It's been my privilege to write this book; my prayer is that it proves helpful in addition to what you're already doing, in whichever capacity you are called to communicate, as you love and serve your communities.

If I could retitle my dissertation, it would be the title of this book:
So Everyone Can Hear: Communicating church in a digital culture.

Mark Crosby

THANKS

I'd like to honour those who helped in some way to make this book a reality.

Anna – you encouraged me to write this book and have always been unswerving in your support of me. This book exists because of your belief in me and what this book could be. To do life by your side is my humble privilege. Your faith inspires me, your love propels me and your wisdom guides me.

Bethany and Levi – to be your dad is the greatest joy. I love you both dearly and count it a privilege to be your father. This book was made possible by your extravagant love, kindness and infectious joy. Thank you for cheering me on.

Mum and Dad – thank you for birthing in me a love for the Church, a heart of service and a pursuit of Jesus. For the bookcases overflowing with Bibles and inspirational books by John Wimber, David Pytches, David Watson and Nicky Cruz. I read them all and, together with your example, they gave me a lens through which I saw and met Jesus.

Everyone whose encouragement, inspiration, wisdom, feedback, proofing and sharing of skills made this book better than I could have done alone. Pete Crosby, Phil Crosby, Jude Bonnington, James Rankine, Jen Rankine, Naomi Whybrow, John Wright, Debby Wright, John Mumford, Eleanor Mumford, Joe Dawson, Mark Elsdon-Dew, Alan Scott, Kathryn Scott, James Dwyer, Jonny Goodchild, Jonny Norridge, Sophie Douglas, Andy Fearon, Rhoda Fearon, Tom Bell, Dan Wilt, Steve Nicholson, Michael Gatlin, Jay Pathak, Rich Wilson, Miriam Swaffield, Simon Ponsonby, Mike Pilavachi, Jono Bradley, Jon Sidnell, James Bullock. The amazing team at SPCK: Elizabeth Neep (thank you for believing in me and championing this book), Steve Mitchell, Alexandra McDonald, Mollie Barker, Mark Read and the brilliant art department, plus all the unseen heroes who made this book possible. Laura Treneer, Jo Swinney and the wonderful staff at Christian Publishing & Outreach (CPO) for your support and passion for church communications.

A big thank you to the Unsplash Community who provided all the photography in this book, with the exception of the image on page 131, which is by Stefan Schurr/Shutterstock.com. We are so blessed to have such great and generous visual communicators in the world.

I work with marvellous people and so a huge thank you goes to the Vineyard Churches UK & Ireland staff, Vineyard Leadership Group and Vineyard Church Cardiff team. It's a joy to work with you all and I'm very grateful to serve alongside such gifted people who love Jesus so much.

The Vineyard tribe, all of you, from California to Cardiff, from Carlisle to Causeway Coast and everywhere in between. Thank you for making the Vineyard movement a home.

CHAPTER 01
CHAPTER 01
CHAPTER 01

WHAT'S THE POINT?

CHAPTER 01
CHAPTER 01
CHAPTER 01

WHAT'S THE POINT?

Coffee. For a bean lover, even the word can conjure the taste of that arabica blend or the aroma of a freshly prepared flat white. My wife Anna and I love seeking out new coffee shops, the discovery of a hidden gem filling us with joy as we soak up our new surroundings. And yet, wherever we land, every café has one simple purpose – although the seating, decor, lighting, signs, music, food, vibe and owners may be different (to greater or lesser degrees) – to encourage people to enter to drink coffee.

Churches are not so different. At its core, a church is a community of people who gather to worship, dwell in the presence of God, pray, receive teaching . . . and maybe get a cup of coffee. The decor, signs, music and vibe can be as varied as those of different coffee shops but, unlike local businesses, a church is not in competition with other churches (or, at least, it shouldn't be).

COMMUNITY LIES AT THE HEART OF CHURCH

Different communities help us to weave a rich tapestry of Jesus' Church, presenting a beautiful picture of unification in which there is a church for every person looking for one. As the world looks to the Church, we need to make it easy for anyone to find a church that suits them, where there are people like them and where they can find a community to call home.

But can we really rely on people stumbling through our church doors or discovering our hidden gems? We live in an era in which communications are the dominant influence and, as Christians, we need to understand and implement communications in our churches in a way that allows us to reach a world desperate for the love of Jesus.

What we provide through communications – to those both inside and outside the Church – should be a reassurance and reminder of what God says about us; an invitation to be welcomed in, to become part of, and participate in, the activity of a loving church community.

'Church communications' means any message that is intentionally (or not) communicated from a church, ministry, staff member or key individual about the church.

Whether we lead a church, a small group or a welcome team, greet newcomers in the car park or gather members of our community over coffee at the end of a service, each of us plays an active role in communicating what it means to be part of our church community today.

When done well, communications is about joining the dots between all that happens in your church, setting expectations for visitors, resetting perceptions, managing the ebbs and flows of church life, and maintaining a consistent, authentic rhythm of messaging that builds momentum and introduces people to the church community and, ultimately, the kingdom of God.

COMMUNICATIONS INVOLVES

Church communications involve

- working with your teams to peel back the layers of what needs to be broadcast over time, discovering the gold in stories, hearing the vision, and working out how to get this to a wider audience;
- filtering every message through your values and making sure that an inclusive tone is always at the forefront of what you do;
- ensuring that everyone in your church knows how to invite friends and visitors to services and events, and how to welcome them into your building;
- making the most of social media, films, printed materials, signs, emails, podcasts, mobile apps and screens to get your message across in a timely fashion.

It sounds simple, but even in blue-chip companies we see countless examples where the communications process falls short. However, wherever it's done well, it empowers teams and grows an organisation. It's not an exact science – every church needs to adapt communications to its own culture and context – but the fundamental principles rarely change.

Making sure everyone can hear is the crux of this book. Individuals hear and receive messages in different ways, and it's our job to make it possible for all to know what is being said – so everyone can hear, and ultimately share, the good news of God.

At their heart, church communications fall into a simple pattern of four areas, which we could label the 'four Ms':

1. message;
2. market;
3. media;
4. moment.

Message: What do you need to say? How can you ensure that your message contains the essential information?

Market: Are you seeking to get your message across to a congregation, your church community, specific ministries, a smaller group or a locality? Identify *who* this is for.

Media: How do these people like to receive communication and do you have the ability to reach them in this way? Will it be written communication? If so, do you need images to go with it? Would it work as a film or does it need to be a podcast? What resources are available to you?

Moment: Work backwards from the event. When is the right moment to broadcast this message, and does there need to be a number of messages with variations?

These four hallmarks provide a basis for the 'what' of church communications, but when making any communications decisions, it is of fundamental importance to fully grasp the 'why'.

TOOLS AND KNOWLEDGE

A short time ago, Anna and I redecorated our children's bedroom and decided to add a blackout blind. If you know anything of the impact sunlight has on a child's sleep, you'll understand how important this was to our lives! Despite the need for this blind, it took me around two months to drill the four holes needed to put it up.

Do-it-yourself home improvement has never been my friend. My favourite part is putting on my paint-splattered work clothes and heading to the DIY centre to buy whatever I (think I) need. I'm very good at walking up aisles as if I'm a frequent visitor and just need a bit of timber to finish building a house that I started yesterday. The truth is very different. Behind my eyes is a fog of panic as I fear someone will discover I have no idea what I'm doing.

The panic doesn't stop there. Back at home, I hold the drill in an awkward fashion and I'm unsure when to use the 'hammer' setting. Eventually I hit something undrillable, force in the final rawlplug, screw everything into place and walk away.

But my labour of love was not enough to hold the blind in place. I was lacking knowledge and a level of skill, even though I had the right tools. The same can be true of our approach to communications.

Knowing the importance of something and having the tools to tackle it are two separate things. We can value communication without being able to execute it in a way that we're happy with.

Every church will already be communicating, but you might feel you need some pointers; you may be starting out in this world and require some background reading; you may be operating your social media channels well, but sense you're running out of steam; or you may be loving your communications and just want some reassurance that you're doing a great job.

My hope is that after reading this book, you will be equipped with the knowledge to apply some healthy and sustainable rhythms to your church's communications and see fruit from this.

CHAPTER 02
CHAPTER 02
CHAPTER 02

VISION AND VALUES

CHAPTER 02
CHAPTER 02
CHAPTER 02

People don't just need a roof over their heads; they also need a purpose for their life and strong relationships. Healthy churches have a vision from God that provides both direction and community.

So how can churches consistently communicate vision and values?

VISION IS A PICTURE OF A PREFERRED FUTURE; VALUES ARE THE FOUNDATIONS OF WHY YOU DO WHAT YOU DO

VISION COMES FROM GOD, CAPTIVATES HEARTS, TRANSFORMS CITIES AND RESTORES LIVES

Communication isn't just about the tangible end product – the neat package of designed flyers and matching Instagram posts that appear ahead of an event. It starts in the foundations of your church. So you need to understand your church's values to prevent the end product from becoming a mismatch with all you collectively stand for.

A church, ministry or group can spend too much time on strategy, and too little on values and vision. We must always put these at the heart of all we do and the start of all we do.

Every time you communicate, you're communicating the vision, values and culture of your church.

We must understand our vision and values as a church *before* we communicate who we are.

WHAT ARE VALUES?

Values are the foundations of *why* you do what you do. Like the foundations of your house, you may not be able to see them, but without them nothing can be built that will stand the test of time.

They're timeless belief systems.

Throughout his ministry, John Wimber would often explain how a value is a belief system that assigns worth or importance to certain ideas, attitudes, actions, things, and so on. Values are sometimes conscious and verbalised, but many times they are below the surface, unconscious and never spoken.

Values come before vision. Once these foundations are in place, once you know your values are solid, you can work on vision and what God is building through your community.

What are the values of your church?

WHAT'S THE VISION?

Vision is a picture of a preferred future. As we paint this picture, we invite our church – or a section of our church – on a journey of God's making. His vision is his plan for our community. It may have specific emphases that we must stay true to, building and creating with this plan in mind rather than getting distracted by the plans he has for others.

If values are the foundations of a house, vision is the blueprint for a grand design. All our communications and methods are consistently filtered through our vision to ensure that we stay on track with all that God is calling us to. Language and culture reinforce this, but the process of identifying and communicating vision is a cornerstone of healthy communications.

Writing your vision down as a clear statement and making it accessible to your church, or the section of your church you are trying to reach, is the first step in making it known and understood.

When phrasing one of these 'vision statements', you can look for inspiration from other church communities, but the only source for your original vision should be God, because vision stems from the calling he has for you and your church. 'People don't follow vision; they follow people with vision.'[1]

A clear vision propels a church into action. God has put something within each person – a dream – and it's just waiting to be sparked into life by the vision that he or she steps into.[2]

Remember this: task creates demand, but vision supplies destiny.

People need community, and community requires work to function healthily, but people also need a purpose.

'UNLESS THE LORD BUILDS THE HOUSE, THOSE WHO BUILD IT LABOUR IN VAIN.'

PSALM 127.1

(NRSV)

VISION STATEMENTS

Here are some examples of vision statements from well-known churches:

Our vision is to play our part in the evangelisation of the nation, the revitalisation of the church and the transformation of society. (Holy Trinity Brompton, London, UK)[3]

God has called us to build a growing, regional biblically based church in Nottingham, which will in a creative and contemporary way, in the power of the Holy Spirit, worship God and communicate the gospel with compassion and generosity. We aim to make, train and equip disciples to be effective in extending God's kingdom, to develop leaders, to plant new churches and to contribute to the blessing of the whole body of Christ.
(Trent Vineyard, Nottingham, UK)[4]

It's our goal for God's love to be manifest in signs, wonders and miracles. The atmosphere at Bethel is charged with faith and exuberant joy, which manifests in all we do. We believe we're on the edge of the greatest revival of all time. It's our vision to see history become His-story as the kingdom of this world becomes the kingdom of our God.
(Bethel, California, USA)[5]

To reach and influence the world by building a large Christ-centered, Bible-based church, changing mindsets and empowering people to lead and impact in every sphere of life.
(Hillsong Church)[6]

What is the vision of *your* church?

YOUR VISION SHOULD BE . . .

Your vision should be

* broad enough to captivate your entire church;
* timeless in its language;
* sharing something of the call and direction of your church;
* speaking of your values through the language you use;
* encouraging action through the words you use (**make** disciples, **plant** churches, **reach** the world, **empower** people);
* inspiring your church;
* looking at the long-term calling of your church;
* consistent, not contradicting itself;
* large enough that there is always room for more, but with scope to be able to see clear progress;
* allowing for the telling of stories that celebrate the realisation of parts of your vision;
* creating an army, not an audience;[7]
* not just about the work in the church, but the work of the church.

'SOMETIMES GOOD IDEAS SPRING FROM HAVING A SENSE OF WHERE YOU WANT TO GO, OF HAVING A VISION OF THE NEXT LEVEL . . .'[8]

YVON CHOUINARD

FOUNDER OF PATAGONIA, INC.

CHURCH CULTURE

Through your communication as a church, you show what you value, who is welcome and what your culture is.

Your church culture might be one thing, but if you get your communication wrong, you'll misrepresent your culture and values as something they're not. This can confuse those who have bought into the culture and mislead those who research your church before visiting it.

Every time you communicate, you're asking people to take one more step into an adventure of God's making . . . and it is your culture that dictates who will join you on that path.

Effective communications create order from disorder. A healthy approach is to spend time with God working first on our values, then on our vision. These are the first two steps in a five-step approach to understanding how communications can bring clarity to this facet of your church and ensure that everyone can hear.

CHAPTER 03

CHAPTER 03

CHAPTER 03

PRAYERFUL PLANNING

CHAPTER 03

CHAPTER 03

CHAPTER 03

The British Army has a saying: 'Prior planning prevents poor performance.'

When we partner with God in what he's already doing, we need to not only *carefully plan* but also *prayerfully submit* every step of this process to God.

With every new project and in every season we should revise our thinking to know that '*prayerful* planning prevents poor performance'.

The wisdom we find in the Bible encourages us in this.

COMMIT TO THE LORD WHATEVER YOU DO, AND HE WILL ESTABLISH YOUR PLANS (PROVERBS 16.3)

In our planning we need to be mindful that values inform vision, vision informs objectives, objectives inform strategy, and strategy informs policy. So our order of planning should follow this natural flow.

- Our **objectives** are a group of goals that sit within the vision.
- The **strategy** consists of the details and plans needed to achieve the objectives.
- **Policy** is a set of rules that keep our strategy on track.

If we begin by planning the policy to achieve our vision, we will miss out the incremental steps that allow us to realise the fullness of the plans God has for us.

For example:

- your church may have a **value** of 'caring for the poor';
- your **vision** may include practically 'loving those on the margins of society in our city';
- one of your **objectives** to realise this vision could be to have a project within your church that 'once a week opens its doors to provide baby clothing, nappies, wipes and baby food to struggling families';
- the **strategy** behind this is the methodology of how the ministry can function for the long haul: 'to work with local council for referrals, source a warehouse to operate from, encourage donations from the church, run fundraising events';
- the **policy** is the fine detail to ensure that the ministry functions healthily and stays on track without blowing up: 'only giving away one pack of nappies per week and three items of clothing per child, so there's enough for every family every week'.

You can see how communications are like a thread woven through each step of this process.

- **Values** are repeated frequently – through language, collateral materials and social media – so that people are reminded of them.
- **Vision** is reinforced through the stories we tell and the direction we travel.
- **Objectives** are made known by taking the church on a journey with us.
- **Strategy** and **policy** are shared through the rhythm of our communication.

As a team we progress through these steps together, informing and collaborating with others (where appropriate) to lean on the skills of our strategists, administrators, and legal, financial and pastoral teams. Only then can our values drip through every part of our church so that God's vision for our community can be realised.

The danger is that, in our haste to achieve our goals, we leap into action and move past prayerful planning and time spent studying the Bible. The story that we tell comes from the truth that God says about us. When we know what God is saying, we have a clear path.

Lesslie Newbigin says:

> If the biblical story does not control our thinking, then we will be swept into the story that the world tells about itself.

The apostle Paul puts it like this:

> Do not conform to the pattern of this world, but be transformed by the renewing of your mind. Then you will be able to test and approve what God's will is – his good, pleasing and perfect will. (Romans 12.2)

When God speaks to us in our planning, it's like solid ground under our feet. As we plan our communications and the story we're telling to the people we want to hear it, he shows us where he's already working.

To paraphrase Jesus: we only do what we see the Father doing (John 5.19).

WHEN YOU SEE WHAT THE FATHER IS DOING IN YOUR LOCAL COMMUNITY AND WHERE HE'S LEADING YOU, THEN YOU HAVE A FOCUS AND DIRECTION FOR YOUR CHURCH

KNOW YOUR RHYTHMS

You have a few rhythms to consider when planning.

Personally, I always know roughly how the year ahead looks, and in any local church you'll have rhythms determined by either the church calendar (seasons like Lent, Easter, Christmas) or specific priorities for each term.

It's often the case that a church leader has priorities that he or she puts in place for each term, based on the natural ebbs, flows and habits of your context; however, these do not always filter into your communication rhythms.

For example, autumn is often a time when churches see an increase in attendance, so it would be helpful if the plans and processes for welcoming and assimilating newcomers are tested and revised for this season; special attention could be given to the language of invitation and the tools associated with this.

Other termly priorities might include: outward-focused events; integration; serving; attendance.

Hold these in your mind as you prepare to plan your communications.

KNOW YOUR PRIORITIES

Priorities will always be present in the life of your church, but in any given season they will be like a pedal that is pressed down for a particular purpose. As we work with these priorities, our rhythm of communications is essential to the fruit we might see.

It's good to know your church's history in order to help shape its future, and also its priorities and emphases in order to inform its present.

It may be that you have a yearly vision talk or that there was one recorded at a key stage in your church's journey. Listen to it; take notes; pick out the main headings. Hopefully, they won't be a surprise to you!

'A GOAL WITHOUT A PLAN IS JUST A WISH.'

ANTOINE DE SAINT-EXUPÉRY

START WITH PRAYER

Prayerful planning is active, not passive.

Knowing that God is calling our churches into our cities, towns and villages, we lay everything at his feet before we start, not because we've started.

God then sows seeds of creative ideas about how to use the tools at our disposal to join him in what he's already doing.

YOU'RE THE FILTER

Every time you communicate, you communicate the vision and values of your church.

So when you communicate, you are not only saying what is happening, where and when, and who it's for; you yourself need to understand *why* something is happening.

You're the filter through which a church runs all it does, so your knowledge of the church's story, vision, values and purpose is of paramount importance for the success of the practical work of the church.

When you know why something is happening, you can be particular about the language you use to talk about it: what to say and not say.

KNOW YOUR CHURCH

The local church is like an iceberg. Above the surface, there are people, programmes and practice. Below the surface is the heartbeat of a church – priorities, values, vision and theological convictions. Without depth underneath, visible aspects will only be visible briefly, because a church without depth will quickly fall apart.

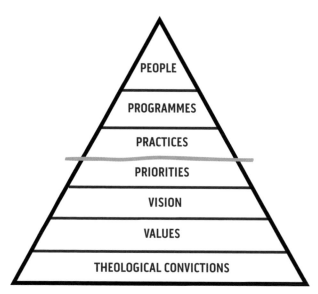

What's under the surface informs what's visible, so a strong church communicator spends a healthy amount of time below the surface, enabling activity to thrive above the surface.

Can you identify what each of these elements would be in your church and sketch them out as a diagram?

OVERVIEW YOUR YEAR

In each instance, we need to be looking at the year in front of us and marking the large immovable items, such as Christmas and Easter. Map out a year, showing the dates when key events or activities are happening, and ask the following questions:

- How much time do we need to create printed materials?
- How much notice do people in the church need that this is going to happen?
- When do we need to put tools (for example, invitations, resources) in their hands?
- When do we launch this event?

Then work backwards from each key moment, putting in key dates when you start to talk about this moment; when you need to start on designs; the date to receive printing; the date to brief teams; the date to launch publicly; the countdown and messaging needed in the run-up to this moment.

You may find it helpful to have a clearly visible year-planner, with each step highlighted. You can revisit this regularly to make sure that your personal planning allows for the time needed to make all of the above happen.

Whatever your role is in this planning, being mindful of what is going on in the life of your church throughout the year and communicating with the leaders in charge of this calendar can ensure that what you are saying is not at odds with other programmes and priorities.

DETAIL YOUR TERM

Based on your immovable events, you may want to find time to have a termly 'deep-dive' planning meeting with the wider team (anyone who will have something of significance to add to the termly diary). Plan at least one term ahead.

Before you start, work with your church leader and draw a triangle, dividing it horizontally into three. Put the priorities for the church in decreasing importance in these sections. This doesn't mean that anything is more or less valued than anything else, but for each season there will be priorities that get more focus and resources.

Once this has been explained to your team (it's helpful to do this before the planning meeting), ask those with the main priorities to submit their key dates; then continue going down the triangle until all dates are in, with breathing room between them.

Next, outside this meeting, follow the same pattern of questions as you do in your annual planning, adding dates when you'll communicate about each item using a digital platform, printed collateral or other methods.

I've always found it helpful to have two one-month whiteboards on my wall (current month and next month) with magnetic strips, so I can write on the strips, move them around and find a pattern that works for communicating. This board is then visible every day, so that my team members and I can cross off each item when complete. If we need to move something at short notice, we just need to rejig this whiteboard and ensure that we inform anyone who needs to know.

What are the plans and logistics that you can put in place as you prayerfully plan?

CHAPTER 04

CHAPTER 04

CHAPTER 04

JOINING OUR STORY
WITH GOD'S

CHAPTER 04

CHAPTER 04

CHAPTER 04

Communication is a vital part of our communities. It fosters places and spaces for relationships to occur. It stirs the pot for activity and celebration. Within a community, the stories of what God is doing emerge, so we use communication to source and celebrate the stories that bubble up from within our communities and the activity of the church.

When we celebrate stories, we're saying: 'This is the vision for our church being realised and we want to see more of this.'

STORIES ARE A WAY OF EXPLAINING WHAT THE FATHER IS DOING IN OUR CITY, TOWN OR VILLAGE

STORIES TRANSFORM LIVES

Stories are transformational. We need to get better at hearing and telling the stories from our villages, towns and cities where our church has played a role in transforming lives.

The story of the kingdom changes lives, and then stories of changed lives introduce more people to the kingdom.

The story of one transformed life ushers in the change for another life, but 'no story lives unless someone wants to listen,'[9] so we have to make sure we think through story formats and use the right occasion and platform to tell them.

We need to tell stories that are unforgettable – to let the world know that God has a better story for our culture and our lives. We don't need hype in our stories; we just need authentic accounts of the love of God that are relatable in our context.

People forget information and vision statements, but stories stay with us for a long time.

WE REPLICATE WHAT WE CELEBRATE

JESUS AND STORIES

Jesus spoke in parables. His explanation of the kingdom was given through the weaving of stories to break down barriers, reveal the truth of the kingdom, make the kingdom accessible, show that the kingdom is near, and offer an invitation to everyone, regardless of race, background, gender or life experience.

God has a better story for each of us, so we use communication platforms to share this timeless truth.

We change cities, towns and villages one life at a time, but also – through digital media – we can throw our nets wide and share stories with our larger communities, full of expectation that God will use our stories to continue the work he is already doing in people's lives.

Stories are a way of explaining what the Father is doing in our community.

WHO IS YOUR AUDIENCE?

Different environments call for different stories. So identifying who will hear the story is a good starting point.

Will the story be shared

- in a regular church service?
- at a church service where you're expecting an influx of visitors?
- at a leaders' meeting?
- within a specific ministry event, such as an Alpha course?
- on the church website?
- through social media?
- in another environment?
- on another platform?

Your audience helps you to hone what the story should be and the story that people need to hear.

A story to inspire your leaders will probably not be the best story to tell on the first night of an Alpha course. A good story to share with your small group will probably not be a personal story meant for key leaders.

WHICH STORY?

Always tell the best story for any occasion.

Make sure you know what the outcome of the story should be.

Are you

- reassuring the church?
- inspiring leaders?
- asking a group of people to take a step of faith?
- celebrating the miraculous and inviting the church to take more risks?
- making the kingdom accessible for those who are new to a church environment?
- inviting visitors to take a second step into your church?

When you know the answer to this, ask yourself: 'What story do I know that is authentic, has integrity, works in this context, will achieve the outcome I feel is right and will make sense in this room?'

Then work through this process of analysis:

- Is this story in line with our church's vision and values?
- How will I tell it to give it justice?
- How can I make it listenable?
- How can I make it relatable for multiple people?
- How can I spur the listener on to take action in his or her life as a result of this story?

GATHERING STORIES

Getting the right story for the right room is an art form, but it's worth the time sourcing a number of stories to enable you to have a range you can choose from at any given moment.

Having a 'library' or list of stories is one of the most helpful tools in your arsenal. I would encourage you to follow these steps when sourcing stories:

1. Speak to the members of your team regularly and encourage them to share the stories of what God has done over the last week or weeks; they will hear stories that you won't. This is not only helpful in terms of providing new stories, but it also helps to encourage everyone and keeps you focused on the direction in which God is taking you as a church.
2. Encourage the other leaders in your church to be passing stories on to you on a regular basis.
3. On social media ask for stories to be sent in. Consider a unique email address for this (<stories@yourchurch.com> or <stories@yourministry.com>) as it shows your intentionality to gather stories.
4. On Sundays use a rotating slideshow before the service to request stories, showing the email address to send these to.
5. Add a 'story request' section to your printed bulletin or other physical materials.

Catalogue these stories in a single document with dates, locations and people involved, so you can search through them easily when needing specific stories.

TELLING STORIES

Once you have the right story for the right environment, you then have a range of ways to share it:

- **live**: shared from the front of a gathering by the host or speaker;
- **interview**: drawing the story out of the person who 'owns' it;
- **podcast**: either of the above, but recorded as audio and edited for your church podcast;
- **film**: either one person or an interview, recorded on film and shown to a room and/or on social media;
- **article**: the story written up, to be published on your church blog, website or social media.

Not every person who owns a story will want to tell it in a gathered environment; some may prefer to write it down, be filmed or have it shared in a different format.

It's important to verify stories so that we can share them with integrity.

Be authentic in your storytelling. Unauthentic stories set a bar that is inaccessible.

The truth sets us free.

TIMING AND TOOLS

When does the story need to be told?

Is there a time when a story would bring momentum to your church, or fit into a season or sermon series?

For example, if you are holding a baptism service in six weeks' time, you may want to tell a story you received from someone who has recently been baptised in your church, so that it inspires others to take a step towards baptism.

What are the other rhythms in your church to which a story could lend momentum? Perhaps seasonal events and Alpha courses? If there are action points within the story, have you given the listener tools to make the action happen?

When sharing a story about small groups, have you made sure that small-group leaflets or booklets are available and that small-group graphics are shown on the screen in the meeting place? Will there be a follow-up social media post about small groups in the week to come? Is your website up to date with details about small groups?

Stories are a way of explaining what the Father is doing in our city, town or village. Jesus used storytelling to get his message across and we need to do the same. How could you begin to gather and share stories that tell of the goodness of God?

CHAPTER 05

CHAPTER 05

CHAPTER 05

GATEWAYS IN

CHAPTER 05

CHAPTER 05

CHAPTER 05

There are only two ways a person takes his or her first steps into a church community, namely by

1. invitation;
2. personal decision.

This could equally be described as

1. motivating someone to attend;
2. depending on someone to be personally motivated.

So either a person is invited by a member of your church community, or, without contact from any member of the church community, an individual does some personal research and comes into contact with your church.

EVERYONE IS INVITED. EVERYONE GETS TO PLAY

GOD IS CONSTANTLY
ISSUING INVITATIONS

In the Gospel of Luke we see both groups of people – those invited and those who came by themselves:

> On a Sabbath Jesus was teaching in one of the synagogues, and a woman was there who had been crippled by a spirit for eighteen years. She was bent over and could not straighten up at all. When Jesus saw her, *he called her forward* and said to her, 'Woman, you are set free from your infirmity.' Then he put his hands on her, and immediately she straightened up and praised God.
> (Luke 13.10–13, emphasis added)

> Jesus entered Jericho and was passing through. A man was there by the name of Zacchaeus; he was a chief tax collector and was wealthy. *He wanted to see who Jesus was*, but because he was short he could not see over the crowd. So he ran ahead and climbed a sycamore-fig tree to see him, since Jesus was coming that way.
> (Luke 19.1–4, emphasis added)

The woman who was healed by Jesus was called forward (invited) by Jesus. Zacchaeus, however, was so motivated that he climbed a tree to see more - but there was still an invitation from Jesus to spend time with him.

We never know the full extent of what our Father is doing behind the scenes, but we do know that some people will motivate themselves and others will need help by being personally invited. Our Father is constantly issuing invitations and we need to be joining with him in all he does.

POINTS OF ENTRY

A growing church has multiple points of entry. Traditionally, the largest and most visible point of entry in Christian churches has been our Sunday gatherings, but as we serve our local communities there can be other ways our churches are encountered. For example, people meet us through

- **courses**: Alpha, marriage, parenting and money management classes;
- **social events**: Easter egg hunts, summer fun days, organised trips;
- **children's activities**: children's clubs, youth groups, parent-and-baby mornings;
- **community involvement**: food banks, school partnerships, welcoming refugees and asylum seekers;
- **seasonal events**: Christmas and Easter services;
- **outreach**: 'Healing on the Streets', evangelistic efforts.

A point of entry is anywhere someone might encounter your church practically for the first time and receive a further invitation to a gathering in your community. It's not the purpose of the point of entry to do this, but nevertheless that is the place where, for the first time, someone may see the gateway into your church. There's even an expectation that he or she may meet Jesus *before* attending a church service.

A CULTURE OF INVITATION

A culture of invitation doesn't just mean sending out reminders to ask people to events, and then seeing a flow of invitations. From your perspective, you set the culture by putting tools into the hands of the other members of your church that allow invitations to flourish.

The culture is formed in three stages:

1. invite;
2. welcome;
3. integrate.

A culture of invitation is not about everyone just inviting friends and neighbours. It's that and having a welcoming church, plus having the systems that allow visitors to be integrated into your community. If visitors feel they are expected, they will feel more welcomed.

We set the culture by fluidly and confidently

1. inviting a friend;
2. welcoming a visitor;
3. integrating a newcomer.

BEFORE WE LEARN TO WELCOME, WE HAVE TO LEARN TO INVITE

VISITORS AND NEWCOMERS

The three stages (invite, welcome, integrate) are preceded by the knowledge that a visitor is not a newcomer, and a newcomer is not part of the community . . . yet.

A visitor is someone who is dipping a toe into the waters of your church.

A newcomer is someone who is taking the early steps towards becoming part of your community.

You can only help these individuals when you recognise the practical and emotional stages that they will go through.

A visitor who comes to a Sunday environment four times is not part of your community until he or she is integrated into your community.

We need to think through the stages of becoming integrated into a community; otherwise, our large gateways *in* are joined by large gateways *out*.

ATTENDANCE IS NOT THE SAME AS BELONGING

THE VISITOR JOURNEY

Going to church for the first time can be a bit like checking out a new gym. Whether it is invitation or initiative that has got you there, you want to work out – but you may not know the etiquette required to do so or be familiar with the equipment. Similarly, a visitor may want to come to church but, once there, his or her lack of understanding regarding the 'hows', 'whats' and 'wheres' may see them leaving embarrassed and confused.

Although everyone is different and one person's journey into your church community will differ from the next, there are six phases that people are likely to go through and that your church can prepare for to make the pathway into your community straightforward.

1 Research

Before visiting your church, people will probably research it to set their own expectations and perceptions. This may be done via your website, social media or printed materials.

Ensure that invitational language flows through all you do, as there is a likelihood that interested people will read your website but wonder if they're allowed to visit the church.

Look at your website through the lens of potential visitors. Do people know how to find your building, what you do during a service, when to arrive, how to park, what's expected of them, how to dress, what to do with their children, how long a service is? Every answer you can give (without being asked) improves the chances that a person will commit to visiting for the first time.

2 Attendance

When visiting, people should be welcomed instantly by a person from a team designated to welcome visitors. Then there should be information provided by the host of the service about the steps that any visitor can undergo to become part of your community.

Teams should be easily identifiable, and internal/external signs for your church must be clear in order to avoid any confusion about entrances, disabled access, toilets, baby-changing areas, children's groups, refreshments, information points, and any other key identifiers that visitors require to ease their first visit(s). These measures reduce the tendency to create barriers without even realising.

3 Connection

After your service, there should be a chance for visitors to meet and connect with members of your pastoral team and core church members, and receive any materials or information that would help their journey.

This opportunity should be announced during the service, with teams looking out for visitors to connect with them and welcome them.

GOOD COMMUNICATION REDUCES BARRIERS

4 Welcome event

All visitors should be invited to one of your welcome events where they can hear more of the story and vision of the church, learn what it means to be part of your community, ask any questions they have and meet others in a similar position to themselves.

It would be helpful to allow people to sign up for such an event so you can cater accordingly and also send reminders nearer to the time, giving details of the location, directions and any other information that's needed.

Not everyone who visits will know Jesus yet, so it would be helpful to have an Alpha course (or similar introduction to Christianity) starting shortly that interested people can attend. Time these courses strategically, knowing where the welcome events will be and how you can help people continue both their journey of faith and their journey into community.

5 Community

Any visitor can be steered towards newcomer-friendly small groups, so they can find a smaller community within the church that they can call home.

Small groups are likely to be a core part of your church, but for some people it can be daunting to go from sitting in rows in the congregation to sitting in circles, in someone's home. To make this easier you may want to have some small-group leaders present at your welcome event to share a bit about small groups and personally invite everyone to join one.

6 Time, energy and money

As part of your community there are a number of factors that help to make the activity of the church happen. The Bible talks about time, energy and money.

Make sure that newcomers are easily able to find a team to join so they can help in the activity of the church and begin a journey of financial generosity. You will need systems in place to help make this happen, with administration personnel working through these weekly.

ONLINE
Research church to set expectations and perceptions

SUNDAY SERVICE
Be welcomed by teams, from the front and by what you're handed

NEWCOMERS' CONNECTION POINT
A chance to meet, connect and explore the church

WELCOME EVENT
Learn how to 'join' the church and meet other newcomers

SMALL GROUP
Be steered towards newcomer-friendly groups

ENERGY AND MONEY
Find a team to join and begin giving

THE VISITOR JOURNEY

HELP YOUR CHURCH TO INVITE

You will need to provide tools for other members of your church to invite friends, colleagues, neighbours and family members. These should be tailored to those you're inviting, so make sure your language is invitational, using phrases such as

- 'Join us';
- 'You are welcome';
- 'We can't wait to see you'.

Ask yourself what tools would work in your context.

Create social media that is not just for the church but could also be seen by a friend of someone at church. Social media is social by its nature, so let's not presume it will only be seen by those in our own community; otherwise we're losing the potential it has to serve us.

Our digital messages can be shared publicly or privately as a tool to invite others. Screenshots can be taken and circulated as private messages. By knowing that our social media can be invitational, we're giving our church community a head start in reaching those outside it.

Printed materials are also key. You can print invitations that are the size of a business card with all your Sunday details on them (service times, addresses, postcode, parking information), plus website and social media links if you have them. These can be stored in the wallets and purses of people from your community and carried around for use whenever they need them. Make these cards freely available every week for anyone to restock if necessary.

Some events, such as Alpha courses, will be specifically designed for those outside the church. In these instances, printed invitations are essential because people know when they receive one that they're invited. A verbal invitation is great, but having something visual and physical is reassuring because you're in no doubt you're invited – like receiving a wedding invitation.

An invitation is not just for the person inviting, but for the invitee. It says: 'I have been invited.'

In your context, you need to prayerfully plan through your priorities and events as a church and work out what tools are available to equip your people so that they can invite others into the Church that God is building.

FRONT DOOR, BACK DOOR

One of our aims in church is to increase the size of our 'front door' to make it possible for new visitors to come every week, and to reduce the size of our 'back door' so that visitors are not leaving soon after they arrive but are instead becoming newcomers, integrated into our community.

The aim is never to build attendance numbers, but to welcome people into the kingdom of God and play our part in his story.

People thrive in community, but there can often be barriers that are accidentally erected, and these may prevent visitors from journeying into community.

Objectively, take time to look at the visitor journey in your church and work out if there are barriers anywhere that could be removed, and systems that could be improved.

In community the people of our cities and towns can join their story with God's, disciples can be made and we can journey together as the bride of Christ.

CHAPTER 06

CHAPTER 06

CHAPTER 06

UNLOCKING
STRATEGY

CHAPTER 06

CHAPTER 06

CHAPTER 06

Strategy, used alongside God-given vision, unlocks a culture of hope in others and points them to a faith in Jesus.

The workings of strategic minds are the unseen glue that restores lives to wholeness. We need the wisdom of strategic thinkers to bring vision to life.

Strategy is, quite simply, the plan to achieve a specific goal.

IF WE CAN WORK OUT THE WIN, THEN WE KNOW THE DIRECTION

ACTION AND INTENTION

> Without intent there can be no action, but without action intent means nothing.
>
> (Casey Neistat, YouTuber)[10]

Our intent as churches comes from our vision and values.
Our intent is to realise the vision that our objectives point towards.

The intent then steers our actions, and our churches gain momentum from hearing about the stories arising from our actions.

So, as you begin working on your communications strategies, ask yourselves these two questions:

1. What's the intent?
2. What's the action?

Planning the action is another way of planning your strategy.
Just make sure you finish planning it before implementing it.

WHAT'S THE WIN?

The reason we sometimes struggle to know the strategic direction to go in is because we haven't worked out what a 'win' would look like for one of our objectives. The 'win' in this instance is simply the desired outcome or impact we would like our action to have.

If we can work out the win, then we know the direction. As we pray through strategy, we know it's there to help us achieve the objectives that have already been set. So before you get started, remind yourself of the win; then think about the direction you need to take to achieve this goal.

MEASURE

When we celebrate wins, we're celebrating vision being realised and the stories that we're hearing. In order to be able to celebrate them, we need to have a way of measuring them.

I've always found it helpful to have 'SMART' goals:

- **S**pecific;
- **M**easurable;
- **A**chievable;
- **R**ealistic;
- **T**angible.

Write these words down and refer to them periodically; they describe goals that should be achievable in the short to medium term. They help to keep us in our lane and dictate how we spend our time.

Remember the definitions of strategy and policy:

- **strategy**: the art of planning to achieve objectives;
- **policy**: the set of details that keep strategy on track.

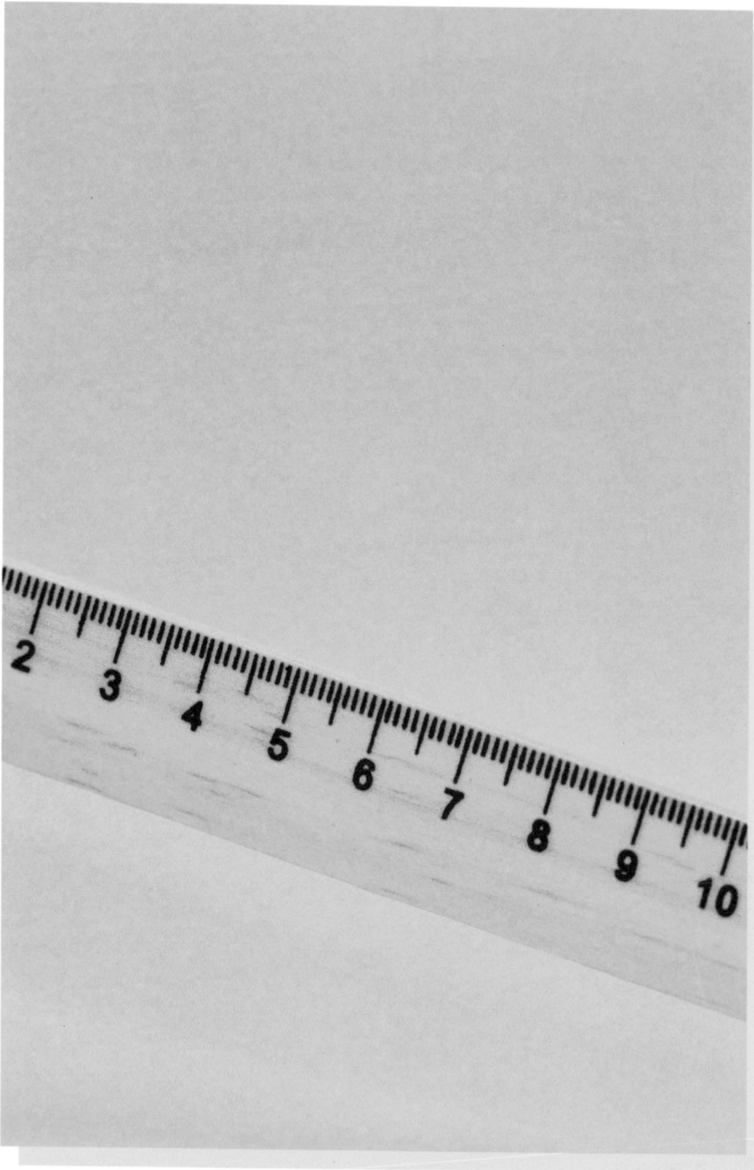
2
3
4
5
6
7
8
9
10

BE INTENTIONAL

One of the keys to unlocking strategy is to know how to spend your time. Here are some tips I've found helpful because they shape your communications approach:

- **Be part of the culture**. Immerse yourself in your church. You'll understand so much more from having your hands in the dirt than from your view in the office chair.
- **Be informed**. Meet with other leaders or communicators in your church. Learn their plans way ahead of time. Help them avoid mistakes. Spend time with your church leader and hear what he or she is planning; help this person succeed.
- **Plan**. Take all you hear and know, filter it and begin planning how this should be broadcast.
- **Know the vision and values**. Use them as a filter.

- **Communicate in contextually relevant ways**. Not all groups want to be communicated with in the same way. Research and learn the best way for each group.
- **Be proactive**. Few things are as dangerous as constantly being reactive. The steps on the previous page will help to prevent this.
- **Constantly evaluate**. Measure how you're doing. Work out why things have worked or not worked. If need be, change things for next time. Write it all down so you become a student of your craft.
- **Be flexible**. You're doing the communications – you're not the fourth member of the Trinity! Work with a servant heart and be flexible as part of your team.
- **Learn how to recognise a move from God**. When stories come in with similar patterns, whether it's by theme or geography, pass the pattern to your church leader. You can be helpful in identifying what the Father is already doing in your city, town or village.

FILTER EVERYTHING THROUGH YOUR VISION AND VALUES

INSPIRATION > IMITATION

All of us need to be reminded of the difference between inspiration and imitation, especially in our digital culture where it's all too easy to start comparing what we can do and what other churches can do. It is important that we recognise and stay in our own 'lane'.

Inspiration urges you on to create something unique for your context. Imitation steals a concept or product that has been designed for another's context and loosely fits it into yours. You'll find that this will only work for you for so long before you find issues with it.

Many of the problems we see in church communications arise when churches have tried to imitate brands or megachurches, impressed by the beauty and execution of their communications. What you don't see in their execution is all the thought that's gone into ensuring it fits their lane.

Imitation is not satisfying for creative types of people, or 'creatives'. It leaves us feeling that what we've done is never enough. The reason for this is that we were made for more. Creatives were designed to create. If you take away the imagination from a creative, he or she will feel dissatisfied.

This goes for working with creative volunteers too. Allow them room to create. Every team needs boundaries, but within these boundaries allow creatives the freedom to bring their own talent to the task at hand. There is a redemptive feature to this which will empower your teams, and although the process is sometimes messy, your teams will thrive and your church will benefit. It's not a short-haul option; it's a journey to walk with them.

A lesson for us all is to be inspired, but not to imitate.

INSPIRATION

>

IMITATION

UNLOCKING STRATEGY

To help you unlock what your communications strategies can be, I want to run through just a few lessons I've learned over the years. Hopefully these will help you when you're working on your strategy:

1. Don't entertain methods or directions that are at odds with the values of your church.
2. Know that it's not always what you say; it's how you say it.
3. Don't confuse how *you* like to receive communication with how your **church or community** likes to receive communication.
4. It's not about doing the right things perfectly, but focusing on doing the right things. You can do the wrong things perfectly and have virtually no impact.
5. Prepare answers for unasked questions.

Our aim with a strategy is to come up with a workable, achievable, measurable plan that works in our context with the resources available, in line with our vision and values; a plan that answers the question: how do we make sure everyone can hear?

CHAPTER 07

CHAPTER 07

CHAPTER 07

WHO ARE YOU
TRYING TO REACH?

CHAPTER 07

CHAPTER 07

CHAPTER 07

Our towns and cities are often vast, and people can feel very lonely and isolated. This is one of the reasons why everyone should be welcome in church. However, if you aim for everyone, you will end up reaching no one. Knowing *who* we are trying to attract (for different ministries and at different times) will help our ministries flourish, while ensuring that we are inclusive churches.

Identifying the people we are trying to reach and the stages they're at helps us better understand their journey, because unless you know the journey, it's hard to know what step you're inviting people to take.

JESUS CARES ABOUT THE LAST, THE LEAST AND THE LOST

IDENTIFY THE STEPS

Earlier, we looked at how to better understand the visitor journey. However, that journey is only one of four steps in a pathway for anyone who joins a church community, as we can see from this list:

1. first contact;
2. visitor journey;
3. training and equipping;
4. mission.

Not everything in church life fits into one of these four steps; some elements flow through every area, such as

- discipleship;
- small groups;
- children's and youth groups;
- Sunday services;
- community events.

However, every person who is new to your church is situated somewhere in the four steps, even if he or she straddles two of them.

As we become familiar with this system and know where each event, ministry, workshop or programme fits, we can then hone our messaging, imagery, tone and invitation to suit people in each of these steps.

First contact: an outreach, invitation or interaction

Visitor journey: visitor to community

Training and equipping: programmes

Mission: outward-focused living

FIRST CONTACT

How do individuals have their first contact with your church? Have they been personally invited to an event? Has someone put a leaflet through their door? Have they been prayed for and then been handed a flyer explaining how to explore faith? Did they see a billboard for your Christmas services? Did they walk past your building and see a sign promoting an Alpha course? Were they helped through your food bank and given a printed invitation to a church service?

At this initial stage, the majority of people won't have done any background research into your church; this will be the first time they've heard of it. So ask yourself:

- What are the ways that people could learn of my church for the first time?
- Who are the individuals who will be engaging with my church for the first time?
- What tools are in place to greet them and what do people meeting them need to say?
- How can I make sure that their first impression is the best impression?
- Have I got all the tools I need from my leaders in order to make the best impression?

People's perceptions of your church begin to be set in this first step. Any communications at this stage need to be authentic:

- your language must tally with how your church 'sounds';
- imagery has to represent your church;
- religious phrases must be culled;
- an invitation needs to be issued that allows people to feel welcomed into your visitor journey.

VISITOR JOURNEY — THE LITMUS TEST

We've already covered the visitor journey, so here let me add this helpful litmus test.

You only have about two minutes to make an impression when a visitor is researching your church online – whether that's through your social media or website. In that short time, people make up their mind as to whether they've found what they need or whether they're going to look elsewhere, or not look at all.

You need to use these two minutes well. This means that your job is to make sure they don't have to work hard in order to find the answers they need.

Try the following:

- pin an invitational tweet to the top of your church's Twitter profile;
- highlight Instagram stories with service times, maps and parking details;
- keep your homepage simple so people can find your church and read about you.

Keep your presentation clear and jargon free.

The same principle applies when people visit your church for the first time: within two minutes visitors will normally decide if they're going to return – before they've even sat through a service.

So put yourself in their shoes and approach your building on a Sunday, seeing everything through a different lens. Look around you: what could be changed to make your church a more welcoming environment?

- How are the members of the welcome teams placed? Are they in places (outside and inside) where visitors can see them and be reassured that they're coming into the right building? Are team members chatting to one another with their backs to people or are they facing the flow of people and welcoming visitors?
- Are there clear external and internal signs directing visitors to where they should go?

Run through both of these areas in two minutes and then get some of your team members to do the same, separately and on different Sundays. Compare notes and work out how you can make the start of a visitor's interaction with your church the best experience it can be.

If you have large events coming up, consider doing these test scenarios way in advance, so that you have time to action any changes and then scale them for larger numbers of visitors.

TRAINING AND EQUIPPING

So Christ himself gave the apostles, the prophets, the evangelists, the pastors and teachers, *to equip his people for works of service*, so that the body of Christ may be built up . . . (Ephesians 4.11–12, emphasis added)

Part of our role as leaders of churches is training the body of Christ, equipping believers with biblical teaching, principles and applied wisdom as individuals, families and as a mobilised church, using courses, workshops and programmes. Our aim is not to replace the activity of the church, but to ensure that the activity of the church happens from a place of health.

This training will cover anything from Alpha courses, marriage and parenting classes, theological study and spiritual formation, to teaching on evangelism, leadership, prayer and how to become more outward-focused.

Some of these areas of training will be exclusively for those in the church, in which case the language used in your communications can be adapted slightly to address the church rather than the community around you.

When promoting activities that are also a gateway into the church, you need to use language that will appeal to both the church and the outside community at large.

MISSION

Our mission as a church is to 'go and make disciples of all nations, baptising them in the name of the Father and of the Son and of the Holy Spirit, and teaching them to obey everything I [Jesus] have commanded you' (Matthew 28.19–20).

As people join our churches and get to know Jesus, get to know the church community and get to know the purpose of the Church, we must naturally look at what it looks like in our context to 'go'.

Which are the vehicles we're using to go and fulfil the Great Commission, and which are the communications tools that we need to serve that vehicle well?

This goes back to the first step. Missional activity will be the first contact that many people have with the Church, so how are we equipping our teams (with communications tools) to set healthy perceptions and expectations of our church?

REACHING THEM

Now that you have worked through those four steps, here are some examples to get you thinking about some specifics for your context and how the principles apply.

One of your evangelism teams is out on the streets one Saturday. A few members pray for a young man with a physical ailment, and he gets miraculously and instantly healed. He wants to know more and wants to come to church.

What's the communication process in place that moves this man from first contact to the visitor journey?

What do you need to produce (design, print, order, circulate) so that these teams are prepared every time they go out on to the streets?

Will they hand over a leaflet (putting the onus on the healed man to take the next steps) or could there be a way for them to receive his details so they can contact him and follow up?

Do the people on your evangelism teams need some kind of training so that they understand the visitor journey? What else can you do to help this young man become part of the community that Jesus is inviting him into?

A family arrives at your church for the first time. During the service, an announcement is made about a welcome event happening after the service the following week.

- How are the members of that family clearly invited to that event? How do they know it's for them?
- What kind of language is used to describe it, and is it consistent with any other literature already given to them?
- If they do want to sign up for a welcome event, *how* do they sign up?
- How are they reminded?
- How are they welcomed to that event?
- Do the church teams know about the event and what happens during it?

The above questions demonstrate the importance of seeing how everything connects to everything else. In other words, churches need 'joined-up thinking'. If you hold events without joined-up thinking, you will struggle to get people to come to them, and you won't build a relationship of trust with your visitors. In your communications processes, think through the various scenarios and try to be prepared for each of them, so that when Jesus issues invitations to your church, you're ready to welcome those he invites.

CHAPTER 08

CHAPTER 08

CHAPTER 08

LANGUAGE AND LEXICON

CHAPTER 08

CHAPTER 08

CHAPTER 08

We use language to explain vision and values. Vision and values propel us into the reality of the kingdom of God. God shows us that there is a better story for our lives.

Authentic and consistent language helps communicate vision and values, while maintaining stability and showing a reassuring hand on the tiller.

Leaders need to put maximum effort into finding the right language and the right words to communicate vision and purpose.

LANGUAGE INTRODUCES PEOPLE TO GOD

BE AUTHENTIC

You need clear language for yourself, for your church and for your ministry.

Language is consistent wording that reinforces your vision and values.

You can be inspired by language from elsewhere, but language needs to be authentic to your church and to sound like you.

You can identify your own language by looking at phrasing that is frequently heard in your church, and words that are regularly used to explain what the church is, who belongs to it and what's happening in and around it. This is your church's own vocabulary – your 'lexicon'.

Once you have identified the lexicon of your church, you need to make sure that this transfers from the pulpit to all your media platforms, so that your language is always authentic and communicates your values.

'THE WORDS WE WRITE ARE ONE OF THE MOST IMPORTANT WAYS WE HAVE OF SHOWING PEOPLE WHAT WE STAND FOR.'[11]

MONZO

STAY STOKED

I recently bought a GoPro camera. GoPros are tiny action cameras that capture footage with incredible quality while strapped to the front of a helmet as you jump out of a plane or ski down a treacherous gorge.

The sort of people who normally buy a GoPro camera are outdoors-focused people, younger than me, more in tune with surf-culture slang where terms like 'stoked', 'hang ten' and 'shakka' are commonplace.

When registering my new camera on the GoPro website, I had to tick a box asking if I wanted to 'stay stoked' and receive the latest news from GoPro.

The makers of GoPro include language like this so that the people in their target market know they're in the right place for the lifestyle which they're buying in to. The familiar language builds trust and loyalty among customers.

BE CONSISTENT

When we have confidence in who we are, when our church knows who we are and what our vision is, then our towns and cities can truly know who we are through the language we use, the platforms we appear on, the imagery we present and the invitation we offer.

Always ensure that your language is consistent, because authenticity and consistency builds trust in your church.

What people see in your digital media needs to be matched with a genuine experience in your church, which is wrapped up in your values because . . .

We use language to explain vision and values.

Vision and values propel us into the reality of the kingdom of God.

God shows us that there is a better story for our lives.

This is why language matters . . . because language introduces people to God.

'ALWAYS TRY TO USE THE LANGUAGE SO AS TO MAKE QUITE CLEAR WHAT YOU MEAN AND MAKE SURE YOUR SENTENCE COULDN'T MEAN ANYTHING ELSE.' [12]

C. S. LEWIS

WHAT YOU DON'T SAY IS JUST AS IMPORTANT AS WHAT YOU DO SAY

BE YOU

Knowing who you are and what you want to sound like starts in the creation of a language 'style sheet' – a document that has lists of phrases and words that regularly occur in the life of your church.

Work on this by listening to talks, and sitting in church and staff meetings, scribbling down phrases that you normally take for granted. These might be based on

- common sayings or phrases that have occurred organically in your church;
- specific language that God is giving the church for a season;
- expressions and colloquialisms that are unique to your town, city or area.

This (ever-expanding) sheet can help inform the text that you use to explain anything beyond a Sunday service.

Remember that you shouldn't have to be an integrated part of the church community to know what is being communicated.

Your language should be wrapped up in your vision and values but be accessible to everyone. When it ticks those boxes, you have authenticity.

When you have authenticity, guided by visions and values, your culture maintains the path that God has set you on.

BE SEEN

The purpose of church communications is to be seen and heard by those who need to see or hear you.

The importance of what is read through external communications (your website, a printed flyer, Instagram) should be matched with what is heard internally (from the front of church).

Your aim is that what is read about your church is matched by what is heard from your church when a visitor walks in through your doors.

For visitors, the journey of learning to trust you starts with simple things like consistency of language between your website and your welcome. These simple but important steps remove barriers that might prevent them from becoming part of your community.

CHAPTER 09

CHAPTER 09

CHAPTER 09

HOW WILL YOU
REACH THEM?

CHAPTER 09

CHAPTER 09

CHAPTER 09

We're clear on our vision and values; we've prayerfully planned our strategy, worked out our language, and become aware of the gateways in and out of our churches. So, how do we now communicate all of this to the people who are waiting to hear?

The method we use to reach them is the ever-changing key that keeps us relevant and accessible.

KNOWING WHAT YOU WANT TO ACHIEVE IS MORE IMPORTANT THAN KNOWING WHICH TOOL YOU WANT TO USE NEXT

RAISING THE BAR

Every four years, I love watching the high jump event at the Olympic Games. I could never succeed in the high jump at school; my brain knew what it had to do, but my body refused to cooperate.

Watching professional athletes clear a height before the bar is raised has always fascinated me. Olympians don't try to jump their personal best with the first go. Instead, they raise the bar slowly, making sure they can clear a certain height before proceeding to the next setting.

Church communications is a lot like this. It's entirely possible that we will look at the tools available and feel sure that we have the skills to pull it off – we could use ten of them effortlessly! – but the key is to raise the bar slowly. Start with what you know you can achieve over and over again. When you achieve consistency with this, add another tool, and get into the rhythm of using it. Make sure that your new rhythm is sustainable before you think of adding another tool.

It's much slower this way than you might want, but it's better in the long run to take a gradual approach. You won't fall into the trap of adding Instagram, for example, and only updating it once before realising that you don't have the capacity to update it regularly. For this reason, it's better not to announce you have a new tool or platform until you know that you can sustain it to the same consistent standard that your church is used to.

WHAT'S THE GOAL?

Knowing what you want to achieve is more important than knowing what tool you want to use next.

Ask yourself what your SMART goal is. Remind yourself of this before you decide on the method. It might be that your preferred method is very different from the one that will help you achieve your goal.

Building your toolkit slowly, and recognising the purpose of your tools, allows you to master each tool in turn before introducing a new one.

YOUR TOOLKIT

The tools at your disposal include

- **social media**: Facebook, Instagram, Twitter;
- **videos**: YouTube, Vimeo;
- **websites**: perceptions and expectations;
- **printed information**: the power of personal invitation;
- **emails**: regular rhythms, invitations, reminders;
- **magazines**: termly rhythms;
- **podcasts**;
- **mobile apps**;
- **SMS** ('short message service' or standard texting);
- **in-service communications**: information sheets, screens, signs;
- **large-format printing**: billboards, bus advertisements, signs.

Although this is not an exhaustive list, it does start to paint a picture of the ways that you could consider communicating to your church.

NOT EVERYONE LIKES TO RECEIVE COMMUNICATION IN THE SAME WAY AS YOU DO

SO EVERYONE CAN RECEIVE YOUR MESSAGE

The opportunities that the Church has these days to get its message out are phenomenal.

Every person in your church will have a slightly different mix of opinions on how they like to receive communications, whether it's predominantly by email, through reminders on social media or from the in-service bulletin you hand out; some churches provide more details on their mobile app.

Recognising that different individuals and demographics have different preferences helps you begin to learn how to reach the whole church.

If someone in your church cannot receive or see the message in the way you're communicating, then you're missing people.

A CULTURAL ADDICTION

In 2018 a report was released by Ofcom that showed the average adult in the UK is spending 24 hours a week online (just under 3.5 hours a day). One in five spend as many as 40 hours a week online.[13]

Unsurprisingly, smartphones are the catalyst for this. It is estimated that 78 per cent of the UK population now own a smartphone, and this figure rises to 95 per cent among 16–24-year-olds. Once you remove the younger and older ends of the age spectrum, you can begin to understand that smartphone usage will reach near saturation point over the next decade.

People in the UK now check their smartphones, on average, every 12 minutes of the waking day,[14] and 25 per cent of smartphone owners use Instagram.[15]

So when church leaders ask me how to be seen and heard in our digital culture, I tend to give two tips:

1. be mobile;
2. go where your people are.

BE MOBILE

Google says 61 per cent of users are unlikely to return to a mobile site they had trouble accessing.[16]

Your church's typical web user is used to having an intuitive user-experience when he or she is online. If people navigate away from your website, having seen that it's not optimised for a mobile device, it is the same as having ten Sunday visitors arrive at your church, but six of them can't find the door to your building and end up leaving without getting inside.

Make sure your mobile strategy is at the forefront of your mind. The same Ofcom report mentioned above showed that 71 per cent of people never turn off their phone,[17] and the majority of time on a smartphone is spent on platforms that churches have access to – such as email, messaging sites and social media.

If we want to reach people in our churches and outside communities, we need to make sure that we're aware of the strength of utilising the places where our culture already is.

GO WHERE YOUR PEOPLE ARE

'We want to reach our church' is an elegant and simple statement, but the truth is that the context of one person is different from that of another. We may know the platforms that our friends are on, and be able to draw up a list of these, but this sample doesn't give us a clear idea about how our churches want to hear from us.

People's lives are busy. Their smartphones are cluttered, their inboxes are overflowing, and our voice is just one among many others in this digital culture.

So, how do you communicate with the people in your church?

Ask them.

One of the most useful exercises you can do is to ask people to complete a short form, either digitally or physically, answering the following questions:

- Which platforms would you find it helpful for your church to be on?
- How frequently would you like to receive updates and news from the church?

The idea is to ask everyone to tick some boxes that will give you a clearer picture of how your church likes to receive communication. This way you're not implementing tools that no one has asked for! It keeps you in your lane and helps you spend your time well.

WHAT'S THE PURPOSE?

I could write an entire book on the purpose of each of the tools highlighted in this chapter and the various ways to use them, but here are some key highlights for each one. These will vary for every church and every context, and will depend on the skill set you have available to you.

Social media
Use existing platforms, such as Facebook, Instagram and Twitter, to raise the profile of your church, ministry or specific events. Issue invitations, updates and news items to those inside and outside your church.

Videos
Share stories and testimonies from your church; highlights from a recent event; snippets or full-length recordings of talks. Explain in video form what would take pages of text to explain, using YouTube, Vimeo, or videos uploaded to social media.

Websites
Consider the perceptions and expectations of a website visitor. Your website is not for the church community; it's for the visitor. It's the shop window for all you do. Your site should reduce the barriers to people who want to visit your church.

Upon visiting your website for the first time, people will decide if they want to visit you and what to expect when they do. Help visitors to make easy decisions by providing the information they need and showing authentic images that will match what they see when they walk through your door.

Your website should be

- a doorway into your community;
- helpful in setting expectations and perceptions;
- useful in helping people find your church.

It should answer a question that many people will have in their minds when researching your church: 'Are there people there like me?'

Your website is *not*

- a cure-all for every ministry's communications problems;
- an in-depth narrative of your church;
- a tome detailing everything about your church;
- the sole method of communication.

Printed information

People in a digital culture like ours still devour printed material. An item in print is helpful because it means we can hand something physical to a visitor as he or she walks in through our door. Sunday bulletins give visitors a short 'user guide' about what to expect and what is expected from them. Leaflets update the church on upcoming events, venues, timings, postcodes and where to find more information.

Print also allows our churches to make invitations that people can hand out to friends and neighbours. The power of a personal invitation to an Alpha course is magnified when accompanied by a printed invitation.

Emails

A regular (spaced-out) rhythm of emails – sent with clear objectives to inform those who have signed up for them – can help your church know what it needs to know. Email may not be adored by

PRINT ISN'T DEAD. RELYING SOLELY ON PRINT IS DEAD

office workers, but it's still relied on by many as a primary form of communication. It's low cost and easy to monitor. Use it for updates, news, invites and reminders.

Magazines

As churches grow past the 300–400 size, the scale of events and ministries makes it harder to communicate. Introducing several small magazines a year can help solve this problem. They can contain important dates for the next few months, stories from the last few months, and information for visitors and newcomers, as well as recommending resources.

A significant investment of time, from all leaders, is needed to make this happen and ensure that the next season is well planned, but the effort pays off, and magazines can become invaluable to your community.

Podcasts

Record your talks, stories and interviews; then distribute these as podcast episodes and update your social media followers every time there's a new talk. There are many tools available now that make this an effortless task, but the fruit from your church will be evident as people listen again to sermons that help them in their walk with Jesus.

Mobile apps

Not every church needs a mobile app, but churches of a certain size may find that this tool can solve a communication issue, especially if push notifications are used sparingly. Bespoke apps can be very costly, while off-the-shelf apps can limit what you want to achieve. Be sure that an app actually solves your problem rather than just appeasing the tech-hungry in your church.

SMS

Text messaging improves the chances of everyone knowing what is going on, and encourages sign-ups and attendance at events. It's also possible to let people sign up for events by either circulating a link or allowing visitors to receive more information by texting in.

A few years ago, my wife put on a craft night for women in our city – for those both inside and outside the church. She only allowed text sign-ups, which she promoted through flyers (printed in-house) and through the church welcome sheet: minimal expenditure and low administration.

As a result, 76 tickets were purchased by 36 different people, ranging from teenagers to senior citizens.

A reminder was sent out by text 24 hours before the event in the form of a positive message encouraging people to (a) not forget to come, and (b) get excited about the evening.

The event was due to be held in a rented room on the third storey of a multilevel building. On the evening, the managers of the venue wouldn't allow us to have a welcome team on the ground floor to direct people to the third. So instead, at short notice, we sent out a text to everyone who had signed up to let them know how to find the room; instantly they all received the information, and not one person got lost.

On the night 75 people came. Remember that 76 had signed up. Good communication from a good leader resulted in a positive event at which 60 per cent of people were not from our church.

In-service communications

From the material a visitor is handed as he or she walks in through the front door of your venue, to what is displaying on your screens (information for today, updates for the future), and signs posted around your church, in-service details create a welcoming environment that helps your community and visitors feel at ease and reassured by what they hear and see.

Large-format printing

If you have a permanent church venue, people probably walk or drive past it every day. One of the most important things you can do is to put up signs that tell passers-by who you are, what you do, when you do it and that they're welcome.

Matched with this will be seasons when you may find it helpful to post advertising on a nearby billboard or the side of a bus, maybe around Christmas, Easter or a significant event in the life of your church.

HOW WILL YOU REACH THEM?

This chapter has just been a cursory look at a number of the communication options available to you, but remember that each of them can be more powerful when paired with a clear idea of

- how people in your church want to receive communications;
- what is possible with the resources available to you.

You can then move forward with a clear focus on what you're doing next, knowing which tools you'll introduce as your capacity grows, and full of confidence that you can reach your church.

SOCIAL MEDIA

CHAPTER 10
CHAPTER 10
CHAPTER 10

Social media is the most misused, overused and underused tool that we have. Many churches have never been shown how to use social media effectively, and as a result, their usage doesn't do them justice.

Misuse can turn off those who depend on social media as their primary form of communication.

Overuse can cause disengagement with your church.

Underuse misses a significant opportunity to reach the members of your church where they are – sharing stories with them, marking achievements and celebrating landmark moments – and inviting those around you into what God is already doing.

ARE WE BUILDING CHURCHES AND MINISTRIES THAT ARE COMMUNICATING IN A RELEVANT AND ACCESSIBLE WAY TO EVERY GENERATION?

SOCIAL REACH

The reality is that as your culture of invitation grows, personal invitation will never be good enough to overcome the natural rate at which people leave your church – through relocation and changing life circumstances. There needs to be more than this. There needs to be an understanding of how we can use social media to reach not just our church but also our towns and cities.

At some stage, most people's invitation lists will become exhausted – our circles of neighbours, colleagues and so on are limited – so raising the visibility of your church becomes more critical. This is where we see the importance of a type of media that reaches into wider society.

As we reach out via social media, we must make sure that we're not 'firehosing' people with messaging, that internal messages are not confused with external messages, and that we're strategic and authentic with our platforms so we can reach the audience we're trying to reach.

RELEVANT AND ACCESSIBLE

There's a limiting factor to be aware of: not everyone uses every social media platform. Some people will be on Facebook without being on Twitter; others will be on Instagram and also on Facebook. Having an account on more than one social media platform does not mean that they regularly check what's happening there, or that they follow your church. This means that a Facebook post does not equal good communication – not if the people you are trying to reach aren't around to see it.

On the flip side, your opportunity lies in the fact that the average person checks his or her social media account eight times per day, and those in the younger age-groups do so even more frequently. Being present when people scroll through their feed is one way of getting your message out there.

We need to ask ourselves: 'Are we building churches and ministries that are communicating in a relevant and accessible way to every generation?'

CHOOSING YOUR PLATFORM

If you want to reach people on social media, it's not just a case of having a presence on the major platforms; it's more about sharing the right content, with the right people, at the right time.

To make sure everyone can hear, we need to filter every social media broadcast through the 'four Ms' in the following order:

- **Message**: What do you need to say?
- **Market**: Who do you need it to reach?
- **Media**: Where can you find them?
- **Moment**: When is it best to find them?

This simple filter prevents you from wasting time, and makes sure that your audience is being reached and that you're maximising the chances of people hearing you. The checklist is not exclusive to social media; you can apply it to a wide range of communications methods.

THINK DIFFERENTLY

Traditional media used to have little competition for people's attention. Billboards would shout out brand names; TV adverts on a handful of stations would tell you that a certain washing powder makes dirty clothing white again; church signs would give the days and times when groups would meet, and church bulletins would have every single piece of information that was needed for the weeks ahead.

Nothing more was needed for churches.

Times have changed, media has changed, attention spans have changed – and churches need to change as well.

Media options are now many and varied. People in our churches, towns and cities are caught up in a rhythm of using digital platforms – websites, podcasts, social media – for specific messages and information. If we are not able to reach people where they are, then they are less likely to come and find us where we are.

The answer is not to blast our messages out in unison on every platform. If we try to reach everyone, we'll end up reaching no one. We need to carefully think through how to be effective in our communications so that people can hear a message of invitation from the Church that echoes the persistent knocking of Jesus on the door of our hearts.

1. MESSAGE

As with any form of communication, social media usage starts with the message. What do you need to say and why? In other words, what is the 'win'?

Scribble down the outline of your message, but don't do anything further until you've run through all four of the 'M' steps.

Include in your scribbling anything that will accompany the message. Maybe it's a link to your podcast or an event sign-up page on your website; perhaps there's a photo of a Sunday gathering that you hope to use.

Messaging sits in tension with 'market'. If you choose the message without the market, you'll reach the wrong people.

2. MARKET

Your market consists of the people you need to reach. So ask yourself: 'Who is this message for?'

Sometimes the answer is 'the entire church', but quite often there is an exact demographic or people group that you can identify.

Underneath your first set of scribblings, draw a line and then write down who the message is actually for.

Write down anything you know about the people you want to reach, including their age range and whether they would fit into a distinct ministry in the church.

If you choose the media before you've considered the market, then you will reach the wrong people. So we need to be sure we know our market before we move on to media.

Our temptation is to jump into media first. I've often heard it said: 'We need to post this on Facebook.' The truth is that it's easy to confuse the desire to communicate on social media with the need to communicate with a specific group of people. A lack of knowledge about social media leads to sending out the same message on every platform to everyone.

With a bit more thinking time, we can reach the right group of people using social media.

3. MEDIA

Where can you find people?

Media is all about where to find people. Which platform is being used by the people you want to reach? You may decide to select more than one platform, slightly altering the text of your message for each one.

It has been firmly established that the most popular social media platforms (excluding YouTube) are Facebook, Instagram and Twitter. The numbers and demographics using each one fluctuate in line with the whims of culture but, as a rule of thumb, the platforms and people have several key facets, as explained below.

Facebook is the news and entertainment platform. Because of this, it is highly valued for sharing videos, images and links. Expect to see higher perceived results on Facebook because of its deeply ingrained culture in which users react to posts, without necessarily acting on all you've put out there.

For years now, it has been reported that younger people are leaving Facebook, but the fact remains that the bulk of its users are in the 18–29 and 30–49 age ranges. What *has* changed is that, due to the popularity of Facebook, people in all age categories are now present on this monolith, but with decreased personal activity.

Instagram is the aesthetic platform, where visually beautiful posts and feeds are valued. It is not a place that drives high levels of traffic to websites but is instead designed around the sharing of images. For churches this can be a place where you share authentic photos of your church activity and the local area, reinforcing your vision, values and updates through short captions that accompany photos. Expect to find a younger demographic here, but not exclusively.

Twitter is suited to sharing short, punchy items of news, updates and links - the shortness enforced by the character limit for each post. It's as much about breaking news and sharing what's happening at any given moment as it is a social platform, whether that news is related to sport, politics, music, localised events or professional activities.

Expect to find the bulk of Twitter users in the 18–29-year-old demographic; numbers then decrease as you go up the age brackets. On all platforms, people's reasons for being there may differ, but they're still there. The question to ask yourself is 'Do people know that our church is on this platform?' Make sure you've told them:

- insert links to your social media profiles on your church's website;
- show the familiar icons on your printed collateral;
- highlight the platforms in your Sunday services, both visually and verbally.

Consider all the ways in which you could direct people to follow you on social media, so that when you need to share a message they are there, ready to receive it.

4. MOMENT

When is it best to find people? Once you have worked out which media to use, move on to the moment.

If you don't think through the moment, then you'll be on the right platform but at the wrong time.

There are key times of the day when users go on each platform. These fluctuate from year to year but have been quite constant for a while now as user habits become attuned to digital rhythms. They may change for your context, but as a rough guide:

- Facebook users are most active from lunchtime to the middle of the afternoon.
- Instagram users are most active outside work hours, with peak times just before bedtime for those who use it. Put yourself in the shoes of a teenager or millennial and you'll have an idea of their nocturnal routine.
- Twitter is associated with ongoing use throughout the day, especially by office workers, but expect peak times around lunchtime, early afternoon and then after work.

With this in mind, you need to make sure that timely content is available when your chosen platform is approaching its busiest hours. It's not that you won't be visible otherwise, but you increase your chances by working with the ebbs and flows of user activity.

Think through the right time to post something; then use the tools out there to schedule your post so it appears when you need it to.

A wasted broadcast can mean a waste of planning. So know your platforms and schedule posts.

ASK BEFORE YOU POST

Here are some questions to ask yourself before you post anything:

- Is this strategic? Does it fit with our vision, values and objectives?
- Is this authentic? Does it reflect our church and who we are?
- What are the policies in place that make this valuable?
- Is this post valuable enough to add to an already cluttered social media feed? Will my church thank for me for posting this, or am I just adding to the noise of social media?
- Does it apply to 50 per cent or more of our church? If it only applies to a smaller group in the church, can I find another way to communicate it? Is there another more targeted social media platform I can use?
- Is it internal business? Will it make some people feel excluded unnecessarily? Is there a better way to communicate?
- Is there a call to action? If so, what should the call to action be? If it's to sign up for something on the website, is there a matching graphic? Is the language similar so our users know they're in the right place? Is it tested to receive sign-ups? Do we know the online process works *before* we've asked our church to take action?

SOCIAL STORIES

As we engage with people in our cities, towns and villages, we have the opportunity to tell our story, the story that God is writing over those places, the stories of changed lives and transformed communities.

If we make sure that our message reaches people where they are, we can engage our churches and invite those who live in our communities.

Not every message is for social media, and not every social media message is for every platform.

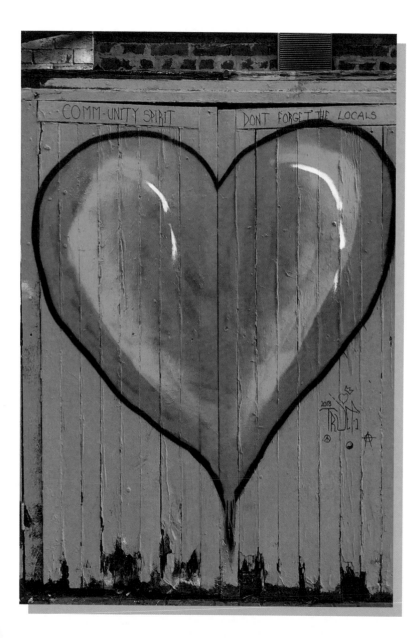

CHAPTER 11
CHAPTER 11
CHAPTER 11

FLOW AND MOMENTUM

CHAPTER 11
CHAPTER 11
CHAPTER 11

We can sometimes confuse motion with momentum. We look at our church diaries and see that we're busy and presume that we have momentum, but what we actually have is activity.

Activity burns out; momentum builds up.

A good communications plan helps momentum and runs through every area in your church.

Momentum shows that you are on a trajectory towards your vision and that there is health and growth in your church. To change this trajectory would take a significant derailing of your activity or a crisis, both of which we will look at in this chapter.

MOMENTUM IS INCREASED BY SEEING VISION FULFILLED

FLOW

A communications flow helps to contribute to the momentum of a church. Our flow starts with prayerful planning and leads to a rhythm of communications that reinforces vision and values, issues invitations to and for the church, creates build-up to events, and broadcasts updates and news.

Our flow is the measured output that ensures we are not firehosing our audience, but are instead drip-feeding people with sustained, planned, regular rhythms of communication.

Over time, flow is one of the key contributors to our momentum. Without flow our communications can either dry out or flood.

Flow is the checklist that helps us not to bore our church congregations, ministry members, or any others we are trying to reach. It sees patterns in our communications and keeps things fresh, but has a reassuring regularity of language, imagery and invitation that our communities recognise.

PROACTIVE AND REACTIVE

When we are **proactive**, our audiences respond with their trust. We need to show proactively that we are seeking the will of God, that we care about his plans for us and that, as leaders, we have placed our plans at his feet and sought his voice for what is next.

Through prayer God shows us a way forward, which we then, in obedience, follow. God always gives us time to implement his plans. It may not be as long as we would like (I imagine the Israelites probably felt this way before and during the parting of the Red Sea) or it may be longer than we would like – as we wait for something further down the track (like Abram waiting for many years to become a father).

Unfortunately, for many reasons, we can also be **reactive** in our communications approach. This is a kind of knee-jerk approach; for example, sending a message out to meet a so-called 'urgent need'; or suddenly realising that the numbers are low for a ministry event and thinking a Facebook post will solve the issue. This is all wrapped up in reaction and response.

REACTION AND RESPONSE

There is a difference between how we react and how we respond in certain situations. Our **reaction** is generally based on our expectations and perceptions, while our measured **response** is based on character formation and insight, and is indicative of how we relate to God.

There is a process of reacting, processing, listening to God's voice and then responding in line with his will, in which our response is generally typified by some form of action – although we know that we don't necessarily need to meet the expectation that is made of us.

Within the communications sphere, your response needs to inform the best route forward, and it may not be what was originally suggested. Knowing the different platforms, the ways you use them, what has already been done and what needs to be done, allows you to respond with knowledge, not panic.

Quite often, reactive communications are not linked to a crisis but to a hole in planning – but a hole not necessarily created by the communications person or team.

When an issue is raised that is demanding a response, it's best to get to the crux of the matter quickly. Ask what problem you're trying to solve, what has already been done, what you're trying to achieve with a communications message. As a servant in the church, consider the best way to solve the problem, but approach the situation with the insight that comes from hours spent on communications planning and platforms.

CRISIS

A crisis is a moment in time when something unexpectedly negative happens, an event that you don't have a plan for.

Anticipating a crisis, even hypothetically, gives you time to make plans, many of which will need to be looked over by the leadership of your church and those with experience in legal matters. This won't diminish the pain of a crisis, but it will help to steer the church through troubled waters in such a time. Otherwise there is a risk that you will take a series of reactive decisions that don't help the church.

A crisis, by its very nature, is not going to be fun. It's an event that you wish had never happened, but being prepared will help get you through it.

Make a list of what a possible crisis could look like and what plans you would need to put in place in order to respond in a timely and measured fashion.

A prudent man foresees the difficulties ahead and prepares for them; the simpleton goes blindly on and suffers the consequences.
(Proverbs 22.3 TLB)

These crises might include

- the moral failure of a leader;
- the death of a significant person in the church;
- a local act of terrorism that requires a compassionate response;
- vandalism and/or a robbery in your venue;
- an accusation against a member of your team.

If you think through these possibilities, and others, ahead of time before there is even an issue (and hopefully there never will be), you can ensure that your church will be able to respond thoughtfully and sensitively in times of crisis.

WHAT WAS MEANT FOR HARM, GOD CAN TURN TO GOOD

THE RECIPE FOR MOMENTUM[18]

Momentum is increased by seeing vision fulfilled. If no one knows the vision, you'll struggle with momentum.

You need to use communications tools and strategy to build and sustain what is happening in your church.

The following statements reveal several 'ingredients' of momentum:

- Well-communicated **vision** builds momentum.
- **Involvement** builds momentum.
- **Pacing** helps sustain momentum.
- **Stories** generate momentum.
- **Realising** vision brings momentum.
- **Rapid** changes can stall momentum.

Pick out each of these ingredients and apply them to your church. What do these look like in your context? How can you help moments become momentum?

POLICIES FOR MOMENTUM

For momentum to happen, we need our policies to be functioning. 'Policy' is a boring word for ensuring that our strategy is on track.

We've done prayerful planning, so we now implement this in a rhythm throughout our term. Successful implementation helps usher in momentum. Our implementation helps us

- to reach;
- to gather;
- to advertise;
- to connect;
- to profile;
- to invite;
- to empower.

We do this through a combination of **direct response**, **brand profile** and **information**.

1. **Direct response** requires an action from the person who receives the message.
2. **Brand profile** involves heightening the awareness of who we are, with the intention of increasing goodwill towards that brand, which ends in a positive relationship.
3. **Information** updates and reminds.

A good communications plan does all three. We want action and we want people to know about us. We want response and we want goodwill.

SKIMMING STONES

My wife and I live a short drive from a number of beautiful beaches in south Wales. On one of our favourite stretches of coast is a river that flows into the sea, and if you arrive on the right day this river is perfectly calm.

Leading down to the river is a bank of smoothed pebbles, the sort that fit into the palm of your hand, caused by centuries of rolling waves.

It was here that I taught my son how to skim stones – how to use the momentum of his body and the flick of a wrist to effortlessly send a stone skipping over the top of the water.

It's this same principle that applies to helping an event to gain momentum.

CLARITY BRINGS MOMENTUM

EVENT MOMENTUM

When we're planning, we need to pace ourselves to maximise the impact of events, achievements and programmes.

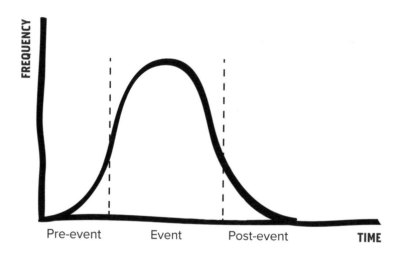

As we approach a significant event, for example an Easter service, the activity and frequency of our communications increases, with special displays and signs, countdowns, graphics, information, previews and details for visitors (parking and directions) appearing on our platforms. This is all backed up by our website, which is kept up to date with every detail a visitor might need, including answers to any possible questions.

Our activity peaks at the time of the event, after which we allow our communications to decrease at the same rate at which they increased, sharing photos, quotes, retweets from those who have been there, and liking and commenting on social media posts from others who have attended.

The end of the event is not the end of the process. Follow up on the event and you'll gain momentum.

Review your policies while memory of the event is still fresh:

- What worked?
- What would you change?
- What took longer than expected?
- How was your lead-in time?
- What really didn't work?
- What valuable lessons have you learned?

Write down the answers to these questions, and more, and include this review in your prayerful planning for your next event.

At each event, we are intentionally advertising our next event in both obvious and low-key ways, such as announcing it from the front of the church, placing flyers on chairs, and giving information in the bulletin and on the screens. Like skimming stones, we are bouncing on to the next event. If we don't do this, we are losing momentum.

Verbally, our advertising needs to invite, reassure and explain, using language along the following lines:

> We loved having you here tonight. We would like to extend a personal invitation to each and every one of you to join us again next Sunday for our next church service, held in this building at 10.30 a.m.

Go on to explain what else is happening for children and young people.

From a key event where you would expect an influx of visitors, such as a Christmas or Easter service, you may find it helpful to launch an event that allows your visitors to explore the Christian faith, such as an Alpha course.

For such events you must make sure that everything you need is in place, so that during your service you can explain what Alpha is, invite people to sign up after the service (easily recognisable teams with paper forms and pens will help with this) and make the most of this opportunity. You may like to show a promotional film that helps visitors to better understand and picture what it is that you're inviting them to.

As we decrease the activity from one event, we are allowing breathing space in our communications so as not to overwhelm people. Then we start building up to our next event, while always having the next occasion ready and announced at the previous one.

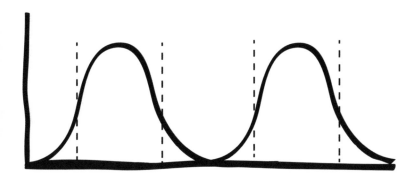

Over time, these ebbs and flows of communication, occurring within the well-planned rhythm of events arranged by your team, help you to build momentum in your church.

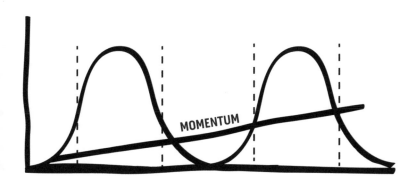

MOMENTUM

CHAPTER 12

CHAPTER 12

CHAPTER 12

FOR THE CHURCH AND FROM THE CHURCH

CHAPTER 12

CHAPTER 12

CHAPTER 12

Communicating to people outside our church means we're raising awareness of the church and inviting them in. We must always be mindful not to communicate internal events to an external audience.

Learn how to plan your outward-focusing communications, so your church is inwardly strong and outwardly focused.

However, not every message is for the world.

Jesus spent time communicating to both his disciples and a wider audience, but Mark tells us: 'when he was alone with his own disciples, he explained everything' (Mark 4.34).

A portion of our messaging is meant to strengthen, train and equip the church. For this reason, those in the existing church community need carefully considered communications that are specifically helpful for them, while not excluding those yet to come.

This is a tightrope that we walk with every message. Is this internal? Is this external? Could this be perceived as being for both? How can I strike the right balance?

JESUS EXISTS FOR EVERYONE

CENTRED SET & BOUNDED SET

John Wimber used to teach about two approaches to church.

The first is the **bounded set**. A bounded-set approach is like a circle: you're either inside it or outside it.

Think of a bounded set as being like a tennis club. You turn up, pay the membership fee, receive a member's card, get shown around and then you're in. As long as you don't misbehave and keep paying your annual fee, you can stay for as long as you want. When you're in you're in; when you're out you're out.

The second approach is the **centred set**. Here everybody is moving towards the centre point of a community, but in their own way, in their own pace, at their own time. There are no barriers to the centre point.

In our case, the centre point is Jesus. You may be closer to the centre point than others and begin to recognise others who are frequently found in a similar place to you, but there is no barrier to anyone else gravitating towards the centre.

It's sadly quite often the case that in our desire to create a functioning community, we create a bounded-set model without realising.

The centred-set approach seems to be what Jesus modelled, often to the bewilderment of his disciples. It's not about 'being in'; it's about having a trajectory towards Jesus.

As a church, our aim is to help disciple people in choosing their direction. For people who don't know Jesus, our aim is to point them towards him.

Look at your messaging before it's sent out and ask if there's any way it could be perceived as being 'bounded set'. What could you change to make external messages more inclusive? What words could be altered to avoid giving the impression that not everyone is 'in'? If there's a 'members' login' section on your website, can you change the position or language of it? What's the underlying theme of your messages that can help anyone move to the centre point of Jesus?

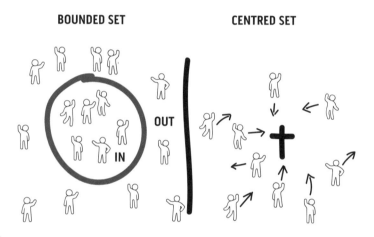

As we communicate, we are mindful that any indication that we are a bounded-set church makes it harder for a visitor to take a step into our church.

The slightest perception of cliques dissuades most people from trying to break in to a group – whether it's a social circle or a church circle.

Through our language, we should set the perception of being a centred-set church where we say: 'Everybody is welcome, whoever you are and whatever you're going through.' Just as Jesus did.

EXTERNAL OR INTERNAL?

Communication is anything that is going out from a church, ministry, staff members or key individuals – intentionally or not.

Every church has messages that are meant for the existing community and not the outside, and vice versa.

External messaging is specifically for people outside your church, designed to raise awareness of your church and to invite them in. It may involve

- advertising Alpha courses;
- announcing seasonal events;
- brand awareness.

Internal messaging is for those who already consider themselves part of your church, such as

- notification of leaders' meetings;
- alerts about team training events;
- weekly updates;
- information and reminders.

There is also a hybrid approach.

Hybrid messaging is for both groups of people, and crosses over to include communications about

- Sunday services;
- other gatherings.

Then the LORD turned to him and said, "Go with the strength you have, and rescue Israel from the Midianites. I am sending you!"

JUDGES 6:14

We have already covered communicating externally to your wider community and locality using tools like your website, social media and invitations; so here are some ways that you can communicate exclusively to an *internal* audience, with a nod to the hybrid model in order to prevent the perception that you might be a clique.

Magazines
Printed magazines can help you to provide a window into church life, informing and inspiring your community for the upcoming season. They also provide hybrid messaging opportunities and offer an invitation into church life. Other elements can include a diary of events, stories to portray your vision and values, teaching to equip the church, and recommended resources.

These publications can be created termly and put out at any gathering for anybody to take away.

- **Pros**: they help to explain the schedule of your term easily; accessible and reliable format.
- **Cons**: cost and design skill may be a barrier for some churches.

Email

Email isn't especially high-tech or complex, but that's not really important. The statistics still say that email is one of the most efficient ways to reach an audience repeatedly. However, because it's simple it's often ignored or not valued highly, or messages are rushed out.

Use email to send out a weekly newsletter that has several functions. It could

- remind your church about what's happening this week (some people will have forgotten) and where to find events;
- let people know what they missed if they missed a Sunday gathering;
- give a summary of the main talk and how to listen to it again;
- provide links to sign up for events;
- include resources that supplement any training happening in the church.

Creating a newsletter template and then editing it each week is a fast and effective way to reach your internal audience and doesn't require high levels of design or technical expertise.

Email is also useful for communicating team rotas (as are reminder text messages) and for sending out letters from the pastoral team.

- **Pros**: fast, effective, low cost.
- **Cons**: if done badly, it can be ignored over time.

Mobile apps

Apps can be a hybrid solution – up to a point – and may include podcasts, updates, small-group information, articles, methods for giving and a full diary. The nature of evolving smartphone technology and regularly updated phone software makes the maintenance of these a murky area for anyone who isn't involved in this world and it can become costly.

One possible solution is to explore an off-the-shelf option, that is, to use a specialist firm whose experts have created ways you can build your own app while they take care of the technical side. Unless there are levels of automation within your app, it can become 'one more thing' to maintain, which you may not appreciate further down the track. So ensure you have the capacity to take this on before promising it to the church.

- **Pros**: relevant to a digital culture.
- **Cons**: time, cost and skill can be a barrier for many churches; an app relies on someone in your church installing and checking it.

Church database

Don't be put off by the word 'database'. This is essentially a tool that

- allows you to manage and process information that comes in from visitors;
- aids you in helping people through the visitor journey;
- enables you to update newcomers (with newsletters, for example);
- helps with the running of teams and processing your giving.

The flipside of databases is that many of them have a feature that allows anyone included on the database to request a login to a 'members' section'; here, people can access and edit their own data, view and sign up for events, change their giving, listen to a podcast or apply to join a small group.

The database I have the most familiarity with is called ChurchSuite, which is run by a good friend of mine, but there are a number of contenders for this fast-growing market and it's worth exploring them to find the one that suits you.

- **Pros**: easily manages data; lets people update their own details; eases administration.
- **Cons**: care is needed in how you communicate the 'members' section' so as not to present a bounded-set approach.

Small groups

If we're recommending that life is better lived in circles than in rows, then we're hoping that we have a high percentage of our community committed to a small group, a place where people can know and be known.

A key to making sure our church knows what's going on is by making sure our small-group leaders know what's going on.

You can then enter a rhythm of giving small-group leaders any information they need to share with their group.

This might include

- a filmed piece from the church leader;
- reminders about training events;
- resource lists;
- news of upcoming events;
- printed invitations.

Working ahead of time, work out what your small-group leaders would need and how to get it to them. This may include sending a monthly email with some highlights for them to share, or sharing information through a group messaging platform (for example, WhatsApp or Facebook).

- **Pros**: communicates to a smaller group effectively; individuals like being informed personally; reaches a high proportion of the church community.
- **Cons**: relies on not leaving small-group leaders out of the loop, which needs a commitment of administrative and pastoral time.

NEVER WRONG-FOOT LEADERS

When we are disseminating information, no one should hear anything out of turn or be caught wrong-footed by a piece of news. This especially applies to leaders.

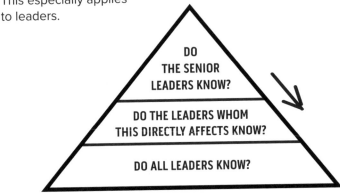

DO THE SENIOR LEADERS KNOW?

DO THE LEADERS WHOM THIS DIRECTLY AFFECTS KNOW?

DO ALL LEADERS KNOW?

When leaders hear news in the order that is most helpful, you build trust (or credit) with them. Often leaders are wrong-footed simply by thoughtlessness or lack of planning.

A leader should never receive a new item of news from someone he or she leads, so plan to avoid this at all costs. A good process of dissemination recognises and affirms pastoral and structural leadership.

By missing out leaders who should be 'in the know', you're hurting your relationships with them, removing responsibility from them and decreasing the authority that they carry.

Include, in your planning, ample time for leaders to hear news in the right order. The pattern of communication should be . . .

leaders ➡ internal ➡ external

GROWING A CHURCH

CHAPTER 13

CHAPTER 13

CHAPTER 13

A considerable portion of overcoming barriers to growth is understanding and enabling people's involvement in your church. Key to understanding is knowing the building blocks that make up a healthy church community.

Traditionally, in church circles, these building blocks involve

- gathered environments;
- life in community;
- generous hearts;
- generous lives;
- scattered servants.[19]

Within communications, if we can understand these building blocks, we can understand how to facilitate a welcoming environment in each of them, and help our church community to grow. It may be that the particular sphere you are communicating in pertains more closely to one of these factors than another, but as they are so intertwined we will look at them all, taking each in turn.

THEY BROKE BREAD IN THEIR HOMES AND ATE TOGETHER WITH GLAD AND SINCERE HEARTS (ACTS 2.46)

GATHERED ENVIRONMENTS

When the whole church meets regularly, we have the privilege of worshipping together. In the letter to the Hebrews we read:

> Let us draw near to God with a sincere heart and with the full assurance that faith brings, having our hearts sprinkled to cleanse us from a guilty conscience and having our bodies washed with pure water. Let us hold unswervingly to the hope we profess, for he who promised is faithful. And let us consider how we may spur one another on towards love and good deeds, not giving up meeting together, as some are in the habit of doing, but encouraging one another . . .
> (Hebrews 10.22–25)

Some things are vital in creating a healthy gathering, aside from the more obvious ones such as worship, preaching and prayer. There are other aspects that you can encourage through your communications.

When you share and celebrate areas in line with your vision and values, you see an increased sense of direction for the church. This does not necessarily mean increased involvement in the activity in the church, but rather a greater understanding of the vision of the church (which in turn should include some of the activity of the church).

So, use your gathered environments to encourage and celebrate

- life in community;
- generous hearts;
- generous lives;
- scattered servants.

LIFE IN COMMUNITY

Life is best lived in community so, as a church, we help facilitate smaller groups of community – small groups[20] – that meet during the week.

Cultivating and multiplying these as a church helps overcome growth barriers and provides an environment for community to occur.

Regularly inviting visitors and newcomers into these smaller groups is key to integrating newer people into community, but bear in mind that it's a huge leap for anyone new to your church to join one of these groups.

In your church's language, you can explain what small groups are and invite people in, using one of the following methods:

- establishing a rhythm of explanation and invitation during a 'notices' section;
- interviewing someone new to the church who has joined a small group;
- sharing a story from one of your small groups;
- launching a new small group and interviewing those who lead it;
- showing photos from small-group activity;
- releasing your small groups to serve the wider community together.

ENCOURAGE EXPANSIVE COMMUNITY

> They broke bread in their homes and ate together with glad and sincere hearts . . .
> (Acts 2.46)

Small groups are a sign of how we intend to live our lives: lives in relationship, lives around the table, and lives where communities merge.

Ticking the box of 'gathering once a week in a person's house' is a good thing, but the bar is too low. It shows the right intention, but it's not the realisation of how God intended us to live.

As the Church, we need community for support, encouragement, friendship, and much more.

Celebrate the community coming together; celebrate the tables that are shared. Encourage communities to merge, as those who love Jesus sit around a table with those who haven't yet met him.

By directing people into small groups, you're inviting them to realise the fullness of life when living in community. You may find it helpful to

- have a map of these small groups, both on your website and displayed somewhere in the Sunday environment;
- create individual invitation cards for small-group leaders to use;
- spread information about what small groups are and why it's important to find one to be part of;
- give newcomers easy ways to enquire about a specific small group or to sign up for it.

GENEROUS HEARTS

There is much to be said for explaining the role of money in the Church, the biblical mandate for giving and how the money donated to your church will be used.

People give for several reasons, and this might tally with their understanding and journey towards maturity in faith. For example, they may give

- out of a sense of duty or obligation;
- because they are captivated by vision;
- to meet a need that directly affects them, their family or their friends;
- due to conviction or the encouragement of the Holy Spirit;
- from generosity of heart.

The apostle Paul put it like this:

> Whoever sows sparingly will also reap sparingly, and whoever sows generously will also reap generously. Each of you should give what you have decided in your heart to give, not reluctantly or under compulsion, for God loves a cheerful giver. (2 Corinthians 9.6–7)

Your language will dictate how your church decides to give, but we need to understand that giving is a journey. Some people will be used to generosity, but those newer to faith may never have been in an environment where giving is a posture of the heart rather than a duty, so the concept needs explaining, as well as understanding from you.

There are five groups of givers in any church:

1. **starting**: those who traditionally give small amounts when prompted;
2. **dependable**: those who dutifully give every month, but the proportion of their income ranges from below 1 per cent to below 10 per cent.
3. **sporadic**: those who give varying amounts at unspecified times;
4. **tithers**: those who give exact 'tithe' amounts (10 per cent of their income) every month to the penny;
5. **abundant**: those who see 10 per cent of income as only a starting point and prayerfully increase this regularly, as well as giving to meet any additional need; this category may include sporadic givers.

Understanding how, why, when and where to give will increase the ability of your church to give.

This helps to foster generous hearts, and financially supports the church.

MAKE IT EASY TO GIVE

Allow everyone to give on a Sunday *or in other gathered environments* in ways that are easily explained.

Include language about giving when communicating with those who come regularly to your church, including newcomers and visitors. This could be something like the following statement:

> In church, giving of our time, energy and money is part of our worship. Shortly we'll be passing around some baskets for those of you who want to give financially in this way. We recognise that many of you will find it easier to give online during the week, so details of how to do this are on your church bulletin and are appearing on the screen now. If you're a visitor here, please don't feel obliged to give; just pass the basket on. Thank you for your generosity, which allows the church to continue its work in this city.

Alongside this, share stories of how church money has been spent, such as

- serving the vulnerable and those on the margins of society;
- running after-school activities;
- funding breakfast clubs for pupils at a nearby school;
- providing resources for youth groups;
- helping small groups to clean up their local area.

Tell the stories without emotional manipulation. God doesn't need a hype machine or the tugging of heartstrings. After telling a story, thank those in the church for the generosity that has made these stories possible; then invite people to give.

When you share stories of vision being realised, eyes are opened as to how God uses our resources. People see that their money does not just go on heating and lighting the church building, but on serving and loving others, on transforming lives and restoring communities.

Some things you can do to facilitate giving in your church:

- pass around baskets at specific points in a service;
- make envelopes available for cheques or cash, so that giving can be more discreet;
- show your church's bank details on screen and on your church bulletin;
- explain in your church bulletin how to set up a standing order;
- give information from within your church's database;
- display bank details and donation forms on your church website;
- insert discreet links at the foot of your weekly email newsletters;
- make forms, envelopes and further information (on how money will be spent) available at your church's Information Point;
- include key information in your welcome packs;
- ensure that details about finances make up part of your church magazine;
- encourage people to give by text message;
- enable contactless giving (fixed amounts) from one or more points in your church – ideal for visitors who would like to contribute but who may (in an increasingly cashless society) feel awkward about not having any cash to put into a receptacle;
- provide links within your mobile app (if you have one).

Make it easy to give and make sure everyone knows how to do so.

GENEROUS LIVES

Our friend, Jen Rankine, often says that a gathered environment is akin to a large family meal. One person brings a pot of jacket potatoes; another provides a dessert; someone has been roasting a chicken to share; others turn up early to lay the table and peel vegetables; those who couldn't come early stay late and tidy up. It's a feast in which we all play our part.

So it is with our church services. Some people turn up early to lead us in worship and run the sound equipment; others have refreshments ready so we can be hospitable; more will arrive to welcome everyone; a few will take umbrellas outside to make sure no one gets wet between the car park and our building. It's a feast of an occasion, where we all get to play our part.

When you observe these teams in action, it becomes clear that to truly know and love the church community, you have to serve alongside them and play your part as the church gathers.

Inviting newcomers into your teams is encouraging them to find their place in your church. Without involvement, a newcomer will retain the feeling of being a newcomer for a long time.

To encourage newcomers to join a team, it's vital that there is a constant rhythm of invitation and explanation in every gathered environment. This should be carefully scripted to suit your church's language and to match what people read and hear on any digital platforms.

The follow-up from this invitation could involve giving out simple forms that anyone can fill in. These should ask people to give some contact details and to state a preference for a team. Include instructions for where they should hand in these forms, and make the place obvious and visible; otherwise, like the letter we all have that we never get round to posting, their form will remain in their bag or jacket pocket for weeks. You could also put an electronic version of this form on to your website or app for newcomers to fill in.

Your process, using a church database, should be clear after this point:

- Send a thank-you email or text message the day afterwards, telling each person that you have received the form and that the relevant team will be in touch shortly.
- Let the team leader know that he or she has new volunteers.
- Make sure that each team leader has a standard message that will go out to the new team members, welcoming them and offering to meet them.
- Once volunteers have had a phone call or a coffee with the team leader, he or she should add their names to a rota and let them know when they'll be serving as part of a team. The new team members should also receive any paperwork or training, and complete any necessary background checks before starting.

You're not creating a system that works for the current size of your church, but for the next stage of the church, when you will have more volunteers than you can remember in your head. You cannot be dependent on one specific person keeping hold of a post-it note with someone's details on it. Instead you are aiming for something that can continue to grow with or without you. As churches expand, we need to be building systems that facilitate growth, not systems where one individual can create a bottleneck.

SCATTERED SERVANTS — UNDERSTANDING MISSION

> For we are God's handiwork, created in Christ Jesus to do good
> works, which God prepared in advance for us to do.
> (Ephesians 2.10)

Hearing inspiring stories is fine, but without a call to action
in our own lives, it's like the fans at a football match cheering
on 22 players who are doing all the hard work. One of the roles
of our leaders is making sure that everyone in the church —
not just a select few — is trained, equipped and released into
kingdom activity.

We need to use our gathered environments to propel the church
into the good works that God has for us.

Every story needs a call to action. The listener needs to ask: 'What
does this mean for me and what can I do about it?' We need to
anticipate the question and have an answer before it's asked.

For example, if it's a story about helping to deliver furniture
to recently housed asylum seekers, we need to offer people
opportunities to get involved. A simple statement will do, such as:
'If you would like to get involved, meet Barry after the service by
the Information Point.' You would then be wise to schedule some
social media posts following the service; these could offer users a
link to join the furniture delivery team or read more about it on the
website. All of this increases the pathways open to your church for
serving the local community.

Stories catapult the listener into a new reality. Unless we offer opportunities to walk in that reality, we stall the momentum of our church and hit another growth barrier.

Understanding that as a church we are all 'sent people' (whether that's sent to teach and speak hope over pupils, sent to a lab to find cures for illnesses, sent into business to bring life to workplaces or sent to an art studio to paint) allows every one of us to mobilise where we are. This is how we spread the love of Jesus into every environment in which we find ourselves.

Mission is not just the organised activity of the church but also the everyday lifestyle of the believer.

'WE'RE NOT JUST ROTARY WITH A POINTY ROOF.'[21]

JUSTIN WELBY

GATHER SO YOU CAN SCATTER

The dream of God over your life is not that you become a believer and help out the local church. The dream of God over your life is that you come alive in His presence and bring life to every environment, spilling contagious hope into hurting humanity.[22]

I love this quote from Alan Scott. There is an important role for some in helping the local church function logistically in order that the whole Church can be released into God's calling.

If we only ever communicate how much we care about our gathered environments, we miss a great deal. We gather so we can scatter, not so that we remain gathered and cocooned.

We must be communicating, in our gathered environments, how much we value the kingdom work that God is doing through teachers, nurses, police officers, street cleaners, economists, artists, poets . . .

Not everyone is born to lead a church, but those who are born to lead a church must release the church to birth new kingdom activity in the local community.

Gather the stories that result from the times when you scatter, and tell these stories from every sphere to encourage and spur everyone on towards love and good deeds.

In every stage and on every stage, our vision is for the Church to be propelled into the good works that God has for us. We want to reach our hurting communities and share the love of Jesus, so that disciples will be made and the kingdom of God will continue to advance.

Reaching an entire town or city with the good news of Jesus is an impressive vision, but in reality the scale of this task is overwhelming for many.

As you share the truth that every story of one life changed is a story of your church realising vision, you communicate something big so that no one feels small.

Growing a church requires you to communicate effectively to every individual in a way that he or she can hear. Good communication has the power to overcome growth barriers in ensuring that all members, visitors and newcomers have clarity on what you're asking of them and how they can be welcomed in to play their part in the vision that God has given to your church.

CHAPTER 14

CHAPTER 14

CHAPTER 14

OUTWARDLY FOCUSED, INWARDLY STRONG

CHAPTER 14

CHAPTER 14

CHAPTER 14

For sustained growth a church needs to be consistently focused on those outside the church communities while maintaining a strong internal structure.

Reminding our church of its vision should be done in a sustainable rhythm. Gathering in larger environments becomes more important as a church grows. It helps to strengthen the shared vision of its members, while also acknowledging that the people of the church are sent out into the world, and that our times spent as scattered servants will all look very different.

Being focused on the community outside our church walls helps to keep us from a religious spirit. Jesus tells us that 'there will be more rejoicing in heaven over one sinner who repents than over ninety-nine righteous people who do not need to repent' (Luke 15.7). So we need disciples who care about the one.

HEALTHY THINGS GROW; GROWING THINGS CHANGE

REACHING THE ONE

To help you work out how to take what you have been asked to communicate and make sure it reaches the person it's for, I have created this filter.

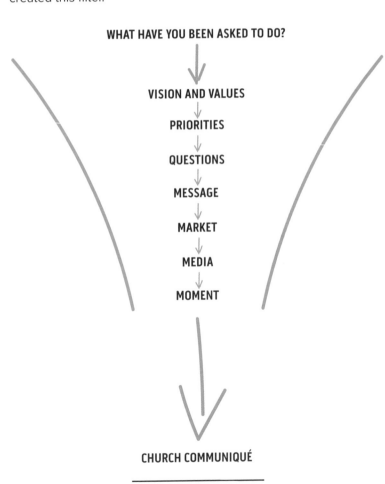

WHAT HAVE YOU BEEN ASKED TO DO?

VISION AND VALUES

PRIORITIES

QUESTIONS

MESSAGE

MARKET

MEDIA

MOMENT

CHURCH COMMUNIQUÉ

As you receive the message you have been tasked with, and during your planning phase, run it through this filter, which asks the following questions:

- Does the message fit with your **vision and values**?
- Is it a **priority** and does it fit with your seasonal rhythms?
- Is there a **strategy and rhythm** behind it? Is it activity or momentum? Does it help fulfil your policies? Does it fit your flows? Will it confuse your church?
- **What** does it need to say?
- **Who** is it for?
- **How** will you reach the market?
- **When** is the best time to broadcast?

Once you've filtered the request through this funnel, you will have all the information you need to create a timely and relevant message, one that stands the best chance of being heard by the person who needs to hear it.

This funnel assists in providing healthy rhythms for the church and for those outside the church.

POLICY KEEPS OUR VISION ON TRACK

When we know our values, our vision, our objectives and our strategy, we need to be just as clear and mindful about our communications policies, as these keep our strategy on track.

Your policy can be stated in a single sentence, a paragraph or over several pages, but it should be written with your vision in mind. Here are some questions to give you an idea of various areas you might want to include:

- What are our formats for storytelling and how do we decide on each one?
- How will we decide on our social media look, feel, length, style and imagery?
- What are the key phrases that we want to repeat?
- What is the colour scheme for the newsletter?
- How frequently should we produce newsletters?
- How do we decide on content for emails?
- What's our policy for deciding on rhythms of communication?
- How often will we post on Facebook, Instagram and Twitter?
- Which ministries will take priority in which season?
- What's the frequency of welcome events and how will we communicate them?
- How often should we talk about teams?
- When are the key seasonal moments to encourage small-group participation?
- Where does our podcast live and when should each talk be uploaded?
- Who needs to approve any of these items?

You will have your own thoughts on additional items, but by thinking through these issues ahead of making a decision, you'll save yourself time and effort, you'll be consistent with your output, and your communications will be trusted by your church.

VISION
DICTATES POLICY

WHAT A POLICY LOOKS LIKE

A policy can be as simple as this sketch, which is a visualisation of a basic communications policy for the process of agreeing dates on which a message will be broadcast, the inclusion of artwork, and the steps to distributing that message.

 Dates for future communications are planned

 Artwork is designed and signed off

 Artwork is stored in the cloud and shared with those who need it

 Message, Market, Media and Moment are agreed and scheduled

   Communiqué is distributed at the agreed times

POLICY NEEDS TOOLS

Every policy needs tools. In this example, you need

- a meeting to decide dates;
- artwork (software);
- shared storage (Dropbox, Google Drive or similar);
- shared calendars;
- email distribution (Mailchimp, for example);
- Twitter and Instagram channels.

As you write your policies, look at the resourcing you will need to fulfil the objectives you've been asked to help achieve – what will the tools cost per use, per month, per year? Doing this will help inform your budget as you request reasonable funds for tools that help to realise vision. You may find it most helpful to plan several years ahead, giving advance notice of how the communications budget will grow in line with the expected growth of the church and the increased availability of tools for any given task.

These tools will help your church to be inwardly strong and outwardly focused.

'Walking' through our policy helps us to achieve the reality of realising vision. The slow, steady, thoughtful journey from values, to vision, to objectives, strategy and policy is designed around being internally strong and outwardly focused. It helps us to work to the scale of our church, gain momentum and reach our local communities.

Policies simply reinforce your values, from wanting to be a welcoming church to knowing the reality of what that looks like. We must always hold our policies lightly, as these are a result of our planning; but when the Spirit of God moves, all bets are off.

COMMUNICATION CAN NEVER REPLACE COMMUNITY

SO, WE USE COMMUNICATION TO CELEBRATE AND ENCOURAGE COMMUNITY

BE EXPECTANT

Your role in helping your church to be inwardly strong should be birthed in the outward-focused expectation that

- God is moving;
- guests will visit;
- they will encounter Jesus;
- they will be baptised;
- the Holy Spirit will fall;
- they will tell their friends;
- stories will emerge from outside the church walls;
- Jesus' Church will grow.

Prayerfully plan with this in mind, and commit to policies that expect growth and will welcome those new to faith.

GROWTH ISN'T ALWAYS FUN

Healthy things grow.

Growing things change.

Change is uncomfortable.

If you learn to live in expectancy, you'll also have to learn to spend seasons in discomfort as you outgrow your experience and rhythms. Being an outwardly focused, inwardly strong church means that you will need to adapt your practices and be flexible as the Spirit of God moves.

When vision is realised, momentum grows, growth comes and growth changes everything you thought you knew, including the feel of the church, the invisibility of what was once visible, the intentionality of your communications and your learned rhythms – down to the number of bulletins you need to print.

PUT YOURSELF IN THEIR SHOES

We exist for those yet to come into the kingdom, so as people begin (or continue) to visit your church, put yourself in their shoes.

Which are the environments that intimidate you? Think of a place outside your comfort zone where you have little or no knowledge, and you need bravery to go there.

This might be

- a gym or fitness club;
- a hairdresser's;
- a mechanic's;
- a new restaurant.

How could the managers of one of these places make it easier for you to walk in through the door?

Compile a list of the ways your chosen environment could be made easier for you.

Take this list and see how this could apply or be customised for your church.

The question is 'What could intimidate someone when walking into your church and how can you make it easier for him or her?'

KEEP TEAMS IN THE LOOP

One of the more easily forgettable elements of internal strength is making sure that your staff and key volunteers can communicate between themselves.

As one decision will often affect another team, leaders and staff should be talking internally to work through strategy and details, ensuring that everyone is in the loop. Beyond meetings and endless emails, there is now a wide range of online 'collaboration hubs', designed for internal teams who may not all be in the same location at the same time. These hubs allow for the simple sharing of documents, and for ongoing conversations organised by project, topic, team or theme.

After leaders and staff members have worked out the details of their collaboration, they (and you) should be mindful that many of these decisions will affect their volunteer teams. You can suggest ways in which a leader can keep his or her teams informed, so that no one is wrong-footed. These might include meetings, group chats, group messaging, or emails.

When everyone is in the loop, you will be able to spend time and energy on moving a plan forward, rather than announcing something and then needing to circle back and pick everyone else up.

INFORM

SHARE

INVITE

INFORM, SHARE, INVITE

One final mantra is 'Inform, share, invite.'

You shouldn't **inform** without **inviting**.

You shouldn't **share** without **informing** and **inviting**.

You can't **invite** without **informing** and **sharing**.

How can you, as a person charged with communicating throughout your church, help the people of your church by informing them, sharing publicly what's happening, and putting tools in their hands to invite others?

In any situation, ask the following:

- Who needs the information?
- How am I sharing the message?
- What's the invitation?

If you can crack this, in your context, then you have unlocked one of the key secrets to church communications, whether you are communicating about a leaders' day, a small-group training event or an Alpha course.

CAN EVERYONE HEAR?

The final question to ask yourself is 'Can everyone hear?'

What have you done today or this week to make sure that everyone can hear? Are the right people hearing the right message? Does anyone not know? Does everyone who needs to know actually know?

Create practical rhythms and helpful checklists that run through these questions visually, checking the church calendar and joining the dots behind ideas and implementation. Ask the questions that fill in the blanks and inform how a plan is carried out.

Good communications exist, in part, to help prevent anyone in your church from saying, 'I didn't know about that.'

As you hone this craft, my warning would be: don't sacrifice the spiritual in pursuit of the practical.

Tools, policies, strategy and objectives will only get you so far. Without an intimate relationship with the Father, you will struggle to see where he's already working and how you can join with him in this.

Our instinct is often to be practical at the expense of being spiritual. We need to use the power of prayer, knowing that prayer has the power to bring about change.

Prayer is not repetition. It's a rhythm of relationship; it's meeting God and knowing him. Greater intimacy with our heavenly Father increases the authority we receive to work in his name. Prioritise intimacy with him. Then, pray as if everything depends on God, and work as if you know that God has given you the work to do.

Spiritual rhythms paired with skilled rhythms will unleash more of the good things that God has planned for your church.

Can you hear the story that the Father is writing over your church?

Our stories define us, so what's your story going to be?

And how are you going to make sure everyone can hear?

OUR STORIES DEFINE US, SO WHAT'S YOUR STORY GOING TO BE?

NEXT STEPS
NEXT STEPS
NEXT STEPS

COMMUNICATIONS
CHECKLISTS

NEXT STEPS
NEXT STEPS
NEXT STEPS

As you tweak, evaluate or create a plan for your church communications, here are some steps that you can take, while rereading specific chapters, to get a firmer idea of what you can do next. Write them down and let this list inform your communications plan from now on.

BEFORE COMMUNICATING. WHEN COMMUNICATING . . .

BEFORE COMMUNICATING

☐ **What is the vision of your church?**

Add this to the top of your plan. If your church doesn't have one, go to your church leader and prayerfully consider what it might be.

☐ **What are the values of your church?**

Write these down. If you don't explicitly have any, prayerfully consider what they may be in conversation with your church leader and other leaders. Read Chapter 2 for more on values.

☐ **What are the key communications strategies you'd like to tweak or implement?**

For example, regular email newsletter, updated slides on your screens, weekly podcast, capturing photos of events for social media.

☐ **List your annual rhythms and termly priorities.**

Include immovable diary dates (Christmas, Easter) and map out these and other dates on a yearly planner. Read Chapter 3 for more on this.

☐ **Make a list of your church's 'points of entry'.**

Chapter 5 has some helpful examples of these.

☐ **What is the visitor journey like in your church?**

Sketch this out from the first time visitors come into contact with (someone from) your church, through to the point where they consider themselves part of your community. See Chapter 5 for an example of how this could look.

☐ **Which tools do you need to help the visitor journey?**

List the tools you already have and the additional tools you think you might need in this process.

☐ **Create a language sheet that includes the lexicon of your church.**

Read Chapter 8 for more on language.

☐ **List all the tools available that will help you to communicate your message.**

Add this to the list you've already begun for the visitor journey. The tools could include social media, all the way through to large-format printing. See Chapter 9 for a list of tools and how you could use them.

☐ **What are the policies that will keep your strategy on track?**

Write them down in order of importance and then create a brief outline. Remember that they don't need to be long, just clear. Read Chapter 14 for some examples of policy ideas.

☐ **Take some time to seek God for his plan for your church.**

Ask him to show you how communications can weave through each step of your processes.

WHEN COMMUNICATING

Before hitting 'send', pressing 'post' or ordering flyers, ask yourself:

☐ Is this in line with our vision and values?

☐ Does it fit within the wider strategy of our team?

☐ Is the language accessible and invitational?

☐ Has this been proofread by someone else?

☐ Have I filtered this through the Communications Funnel?

☐ Is this consistent with our language and imagery?

☐ Is there a 'call to action'? If so, have I thought through and implemented the steps necessary for this to be 'actioned' effortlessly?

- ☐ Is there adequate space between communications (past and future) to allow breathing room?

- ☐ Is this an internal message or external?

- ☐ Could this message be perceived as a 'bounded-set' approach? What could I do to change the language, platform or format so that it reflects a 'centred-set' approach?

- ☐ Are all our leaders and teams in the loop (those who need to be) before this goes out?

- ☐ Will everyone who needs to know actually know?

  If the answer to any of these is no, then solve that question before commiting to the communication.

NOTES

1. John Mumford
2. Andy Fearon
3. <https://www.htb.org/our-story>
4. <https://trentvineyard.org/vision/>
5. <https://www.bethel.com/about/>
6. <https://hillsong.com/vision/>
7. John Wright, National Director, Vineyard Churches UK & Ireland, Hub training session on vision
8. Yvon Chouinard, *Let My People Go Surfing: The education of a reluctant businessman* (New York: Penguin, rev. edn, 2016), p. 47
9. J. K. Rowling
10. <https://www.youtube.com/watch?v=m3TNhDwkL-Y>
11. <https://twitter.com/monzo/status/978670736020787201>
12. From Corey Latta, *C. S. Lewis and the Art of Writing: What the essayist, poet, novelist, literary critic, apologist, memoirist, theologian teaches us about the life and craft of writing* (Eugene, OR.: Cascade Books, 2016), p. 4
13. <https://www.ofcom.org.uk/about-ofcom/latest/features-and-news/decade-of-digital-dependency>
14. <https://www.telegraph.co.uk/news/2018/08/01/decade-smartphones-now-spend-entire-day-every-week-online/>
15. <https://www.emarketer.com/content/emarketer-unveils-first-ever-worldwide-instagram-forecast>

16. <https://www.mckinsey.com/business-functions/marketing-and-sales/our-insights/why-marketers-should-keep-sending-you-emails>

17. <https://www.ofcom.org.uk/about-ofcom/latest/features-and-news/decade-of-digital-dependency>

18. This section is inspired by John Wright's teaching. See note 7.

19. For more on this, see Alan Scott's excellent book *Scattered Servants: Unleashing the Church to bring life to the city* (Colorado Springs, CO: David C. Cook, 2018)

20. Also known as house groups, home groups and cell groups (and by 101 other names)

21. <https://www.telegraph.co.uk/news/religion/10176190/Archbishop-Justin-Welby-I-was-embarrassed.-It-was-like-getting-measles.html>

22. Scott, *Scattered Servants*, p. 45

A SPACE FOR IDEAS